404 and the Marsh Creek Farmer

Confession of the Marsh Creek Farmer

by

F.A. Burnier

to Wayne

enjoy

Fran Burnier

DORRANCE PUBLISHING CO., INC.
PITTSBURGH, PENNSYLVANIA 15222

The opinions expressed herein are not necessarily those of the publisher.

ISBN # 0-8059-4663-2
Printed in the United States of America

First Printing

For information or to order additional books, please write:
Dorrance Publishing Co., Inc.
643 Smithfield Street
Pittsburgh, Pennsylvania 15222
U.S.A.

Contents

Acknowledgements

I would like to credit the following people who had a significant influence on my decision to publish this book.

Professor James Hall from Roosevelt University, who instilled the confidence to attempt such a task.

Nancy Arnier, who read and critiqued the first three chapters.

Esther Jacobson, who copied the manuscript to send to Dorrance Publishing Co., Inc.

And Pat Rogers, who read the entire manuscript and said, "Go for it."

Chapter One

A Canoe Trip

On January 12, 1989, at 5:20 A.M., I got up to do what most men my age are called by nature to do at such an untimely hour. At exactly 5:25 A.M. I decided to start this book. It was not the first time I had thought of writing a book. In fact I had even boasted about my plan. I thought of names for it such as, "If You Can't Make It As a Garbage Man, Don't Try Farming," or "One Man's Fight Against the Army Corps of Engineers." Making up titles was fun, but I really do not like to write. With my limited vocabulary and shaky spelling skills, I knew it would take a patient person to correct the errors. On the other hand, Professor James Hall at Roosevelt University had said he liked my straightforward style, and certainly I must still have it. What I also had was a real story which needed to be told.

It all started—well, I guess it really started when man first left the Garden of Eden, but that would have been a bit too much for me to cover in a book, so to begin I chose a point in my life just after I moved to Pennsylvania.

It was a lovely, late spring morning when my wife Mary and I decided to take a canoe trip down Marsh Creek. We had some rain recently and even though the creek was not very high it looked as if we could put in at the Webster Road bridge and float down to Pine Creek with very little effort. Mary went about packing and I strapped the canoe onto the station wagon. Everything was green and fresh in Pennsylvania. The birds were chirping and the cows were lying down chewing their cud—except for Agnes, of course. I mused on how any living creature could eat as much as that cow. I would swear she was half dinosaur. Even though our farm was a hillside farm with mediocre pasture land, she had plenty to eat.

1

We were just getting into this living-off-the-land stuff, and she only had one other cow, four calves, two horses, two pigs, and forty-eight chickens with which to compete for food. Agnes won the competition.

I could hear Mary reading off her checklist: sandwiches, apples, oranges, iced tea, brownies, napkins, paper cups, hats, and bug spray. We had done some canoeing in Wisconsin and Mary was drawing on that experience to stock up for the trip.

"Do you want to take the glasses?" she called out the kitchen window.

I knew she meant the binoculars and I remembered how frustrating it had been for us when we tried to identify the birds along the Totagatic River. We had limited birding experience, and we would float by the birds before we could get our book opened and identify what we were seeing.

"Yes, take them," I answered.

"Do you know where the bird book is?" she asked.

"I think it is in the car, I'll look," I replied.

The book was just where I expected it to be, and I sat down to think about our day. We had decided to leave the canoe at the Webster Road Bridge and take the Olds on down to Pine Creek and ride back in the Honda. Whenever I am expecting to have a good time, I get a little anxious to get started, so I told Mary, "Pick me up at Pine Creek."

"Take the paddles and seat cushions and I'll take the food," she commanded gently.

"Okay" I said, and off I went.

When I stopped to drop off the canoe, I checked the water level again. *This will be great,* I thought as I looked at the gravel bar just below Heise Run. There was just enough water to pick a way through the shallow spots.

I had just parked the wagon at Pine Creek and was halfway to the launch ramp when Mary drove up.

"I was just checking the ramp," I said. "There is no way we can miss this. Let's go."

Driving back to Webster Road, we kept looking over to the creek to see how much it meandered on its way.

"How long do you think it will take us?" Mary asked.

"I'm not sure, but who cares anyway?" I carelessly replied.

"I'd like to be home when the kids get home from school."

"That's six hours from now. It can't take us that long," I said confidently.

We parked the car and loaded the canoe. Mary climbed in and I pushed off into the creek. The current caught the front of the canoe and it swung around as I scrambled in. I felt like the captain of the football team who just won the coin toss before the biggest game of the year. My clenched fist went into the air and I shouted, "We're off!"

"Shhh...what's that? Shhh...look at that bird."

I looked up and watched a bluish bird settle on a tree limb about fifty yards downstream. Gently, I assisted the leisurely current with three strokes of the paddle and reached for my field glasses.

"There it goes," Mary cried. "Did you see it?"

"Not with my glasses, but I'm sure it wasn't a blue jay." It flew downstream and found another tree limb overhanging the creek. After some discussion, we concluded it must have been a belted kingfisher, but our attention was quickly drawn to a view of a great blue heron standing like a statue in a shallow pool behind a bush. Both Mary and I froze every part of our bodies except our eyeballs, and believe it or not, we floated by that bird not more than fifteen feet away.

"Did you see that?" Mary whispered as she exhaled the breath she had stored for the last forty-five seconds.

"Yes, amazing isn't it?" I said quietly.

During this time, the kingfisher had sought out still another perch ahead of us. By the time our friend, as we had begun to call him, had circled round and flown nonstop back up stream, we had spotted a doe and her fawn sipping at the edge of the water and a pair of muskrats swimming near the bank. A little furry guy we decided must have been a mink or an otter had also made an appearance.

"Trouble ahead," Mary announced and indicated with a flip of her head. A large tree lay partially submerged across the creek in front of us. As we approached, we headed for the only place we could see water flowing over the trunk. The bow bumped up and the canoe came to a halt with about six inches hanging over the tree trunk. Showing great reflexes, Mary grabbed a branch for balance, but because there wasn't much of a current, I told her to crawl back in the canoe so we could teeter it back and forth and move it slowly over the log. Without letting go of the branch, she worked her way to the middle of the canoe as the canoe edged further over the tree. I joined her there, kissed her ear, and told her to get back in the front. Once she was settled, I supported myself on the branch and nudged the canoe forward until it was in position for me to sit down. I sat down, gave one last push on the branch, and we were floating again.

Not very much later Mary's concerned voice called out again. "Big trouble ahead this time!"

Sure enough, strung across the entire creek was a tangle of trees, sticks, and debris. This was more than a challenge—it was disgusting. I felt tired inside.

Mary had already asked several times if I was hungry, so I decided that we might as well stop and eat lunch right there. The grass was too high on the bank, so we sat in the canoe and ate our lunch, marveling at how visible the wildlife was from a canoe, even though there were times we were within ten yards of the road and could hear the traffic.

After devouring two sandwiches, an apple, two cups of tea, and a brownie, I was content and told Mary I would save the orange for later. All that was left in the food bag were a couple of brownies, the oranges, a few napkins and unused cups, and a nearly empty Thermos bottle. Mary gathered up our used wrappers and cups and stowed them away in the food bag and we were ready to figure out our next move.

I helped her climb up the bank and started handing her things from the canoe. Soon all that was left was the bug spray, a soaking wet cap, the bailing bottle, and me. I dug a spot for my foot in the bank, pushed the nose of the canoe up on the dam, and lunged for the grass. I could feel the roots of the grass begin to break loose and I gave a cry for help. Mary dropped the cushions, oars, and bags she had gathered up and grabbed my arm. As my position on the bank stabilized, I began wishing my stomach wasn't so full. I couldn't get much push from my feet and I had to shift my weight from elbow to elbow and tack up the bank by rolling back and forth on my belly. I finally made it, but I had to rest before I could attempt to drag out the canoe.

My strength returned and I pulled up the canoe and lifted it over my head. It was at that moment Mary said charmingly, "You go first. There may be snakes in that grass."

I studied the tall grass that lay before us and concluded I would probably not be able to keep my balance if I carried the canoe over my head and tried walking through it. If there were snakes slithering around, I would be in a very defenseless posture. I reasoned that if I were to drag the canoe, the grass would mat down and make a path for Mary, so that is what I did. It must have been what the natives call scratch grass because by the time we went around and below the trash dam, my arms were laced with welts. We found an animal path going down the bank and used it to launch the canoe.

"I hope we don't have to do that again," Mary said, and I nodded in agreement as we shoved off, scraping the bottom in the shallow water. We pushed with our paddles over a couple of gravel bars before we were back in water deep enough to float free. As we moved down the creek, we noticed more and more junk—refrigerators, washing machines, and more. There were numerous trees we worked under, around, over, and through, dodging the plastic bottles and garbage caught in and around them. We came to another dam of trash; it was smaller than the first but we still had to portage around it.

Back in the canoe, we stowed the field glasses and started paddling with purpose to make up the lost time. The next obstacle we encountered was an automobile with a big tractor tire and wheel protruding from the broken-out windshield. We passed two more cars: one upside-down and the other with only its trunk and rear end sticking up out of the water. Long before we arrived at the Pine Creek launch site, we were thoroughly disgusted and disillusioned. What had started as a joyous leisure trip down the river had turned into a struggle through the obstacle course of garbage to reach our destination. I later learned that Shippen Township had never cleaned their part of the creek after the Agnes storm in 1972.

Chapter Two

The New Lifestyle

I was in the garden picking Japanese beetles off the beans. I had learned that if you get them early in the morning, they are lethargic and it's possible to pick one off a leaf without the others on the same leaf flying away. I dropped them in a five-quart ice cream pail which held an inch or two of water. They were already riding piggy back on the water and I had been down only three rows. Our garden took a great deal of time. We did not use pesticides of any kind and there were always bugs and weeds on which to work. It is my belief that it is not necessary to eliminate the pests, just control them.

I love to watch nature at work in my garden. There were a couple of chipping sparrows working on the end of the row of potatoes. We had frogs and snakes working in the garden too. I'm not much for reading, but Mary reads a lot of books on natural gardens and tells me some bugs are good and some are bad, and when you kill the bad ones with chemicals you kill the good ones too. I know I had been picking potato beetle larvae for two or three days when suddenly they dried up. I guess it was a case of the good bug getting a bad bug!

I tried feeding the beetles to the chickens but they ignored them. That surprised me, because chickens will eat almost anything; they even catch flies in flight. Gathering the eggs in the ice cream pail, I made my way back to the house and told Mary I was going to let nature work the garden for a while. I got out my field glasses and started looking for the chipping sparrows in the garden—that was when I saw nature at work. Crouched in the rows of potatoes, ready to pounce, was Yuba, our cat, eyeing the chipping sparrows.

Mary was making cottage cheese, and she told me to give the

whey to the pigs. Besides making cheese with the milk, we always skimmed the cream off to make butter. We figured it out one day: at the cost of dairy products at the store, we made only $1.25 an hour in our milking operation, but I also figured that if I hadn't been working around the farm, I'd be playing golf or bowling. Adding the money I saved by staying home made the operation a little more respectable.

Our pigs really had a good life. They may have eaten more zucchini and summer squash than most pigs, but Mary cut it up and cooked it with table scraps and grease. They ate it just as pigs eat anything. We had one white pig and one black one, so we called them Salt and Pepper. The cows are Agnes and Daphne, and the calves are Tuffy, Double, Trouble, and Edward. The horses we call Tika and Joe. We don't give the chickens names.

On the way to feed the pigs, I passed the evaporator, which represents the luxury of our labor. Our sugar bush is on the side of a steep hill. It is really quite a task to drill all those maple trees, string the tubing down to the house, and boil the sap into syrup. But once you taste pure maple syrup on pancakes, ice cream, or oatmeal, you are never again satisfied with the store-bought syrup.

Tofu, our dog, had gone with me to the garden, to the chicken pen, to the house, and to the pig pen, but now she took off ahead of me on her way back to the house. Don Lindsey was driving up the driveway and Tofu had to let him know he was on our land. Don was from the Soil Conversation office and he was going to give us some information on a pond. Mary likes to fish, and in her books they claim that farm ponds can produce more food per acre than growing crops. After Tofu and Don got acquainted, we started walking toward the barnyard. I could see Don scanning the hillsides and I told him I thought we might put a pond right close to the house so we could just walk over and fish and swim without making a big trip out of it. He seemed to ignore what I said and wanted to know where our property lines were.

We had gone through the gate in the electric fence, and Joe came trotting over and grabbed at Don's cap. Don ducked to the side and caught his cap as it fell from his head. I hollered at Joe to go away and he galloped off.

"I'm sorry," I said, "Joe seems to have this thing for eating hats, but he wasn't trying to bite you."

Don laughed, "I love it!" but I wasn't sure exactly what he meant by it.

Don had a little gadget he held up to his eye as he said, "You have a pretty big slope here."

It looked about level to me, but I guess the steepness of the surrounding land had distorted my vision. He went on to talk about what kind of a pond would require a permit and what kind would not. He said, "If you incorporate the pond into the run you will need a permit, but you can dig a pond without one." He also said that with the type of soil I had, I would have to seal the bottom of the pond in some way. It didn't seem as if there was any inexpensive way of doing it. Don offered to price some liners and some bentonite and get back to me. Then he told me if I wanted to have him work up a farm plan he could, and if time permitted, he would come out and evaluate my entire land and make recommendations on developing the land for raising my livestock. I told him I was thankful he came out and advised me about a pond but I didn't want to impose on him any further. He assured me it was his job and he was supposed to advise farmers on the best use of their land.

I could not believe him when he told me my pasture was beginning to be overgrazed. It had been over a month since we had gone on the canoe trip, and we had not had much rain since. As I looked around, I could see the pasture had quite a bit of short grass. There were plenty of tufts of grass six or eight inches high and the farther off you looked, the less you could see the short grass. Don explained that the livestock had been eating what they liked best, and in the early part of the year that was not so bad but now the good grass was getting too short and needed some time to grow back. I looked at Agnes. She looked as if she were two weeks late giving birth to twins as she nibbled away on the short grass. Once in a while she would take a clump from the tall tufts, but then she would go back to nibbling.

Don said if I would divide my pasture so I could rotate the feeding area, they would eat it more evenly and the pasture could rejuvenate. He seemed to know what he was talking about and had different names for the short grass and the tall grass. He used terms like paddocks for dividing the pastures and had about six names for the grasses on which we stood. He started to introduce me to them, but even though he pointed out how to identify them, I could not absorb it all at once. I thought there was grass and there were dandelions, and other than that, who cared? Don convinced me I could profit from his expertise and because he was paid by tax money, it would not cost me anything if he worked up a plan for my farm. He said I would have to sign the request for assistance form. I told him I did not move here from Chicago to go on welfare and that if I could not afford to pay for his services, I would do without them. He gave me what sounded like a high-pressure sales pitch, and told me if I did not sign it that day, it would be another month before he could get it approved. He might have other more important things to do then and might not be able to work on my plan for a long time. Finally he convinced me to sign the form.

In a couple of days, Don was back and we explored the farm. We drove up to the fifty-six acres on top of the hill and got out of the car. Don reached down and grabbed a piece of grass. "This is birdsfoot trefoil," he said as he gave it a little twist with his fingers. "See the bird's foot?" Sure enough, the way he was holding the grass, it looked as if he had a miniature chicken by the leg with just its foot sticking up.

I explained to him where I thought the boundary lines were and we drove back to the house. Don got out a photo map of my farm and started drawing boundary lines and fences on it. It was not hard at all to see the lines on the photo. Don said the brush had grown up a little since that photo had been taken. We talked a little bit about what I would like to do with the land, and Don gathered his map and that little eye gadget he had been looking through while we were out on the farm. I guess he saw me looking at it, so he said, "You have a lot of slope to your land."

Within a week I had a little booklet showing how I could get three more cows and still not have to buy any hay if I used good management of my land and bought grain for the horses. It had recommendations for lime and fertilizer and how to fence the pasture. It said I should develop a spring on the hillside so the cows could drink from it, making every paddock accessible to water. I was really impressed with the booklet even though I did not understand many of the technical terms.

I started going to see my neighbor, Thornton. I made a deal to clean his barn drops three times a week in exchange for milk and advice. Most of the barn was serviced by an automatic cleaner, but one end had a drop which had to be cleaned with hand tools. It was a toss-up as to whether that was easier than milking my own cows by hand, but I did it mostly for the experience and advice. Daphne had gone dry, and when Donald was born I just let nature do its thing rather than start back in milking by hand. When Agnes freshened, her calf was born dead, but I bought Hazel, a newborn calf, at the auction and was able to get Agnes to adopt it.

It had been almost a year since Don Lindsey had made up my farm plan. I had Agway put on the lime and fertilizer but the driver would not go on the steep slopes. I fenced off the paddocks in the pasture. Don had told me to develop the spring by digging a herringbone of ditches, putting stones and perforated pipe in them and making a concrete tank where the water could be collected.

Instead, I dug a little hole and put an old perforated washtub in the bottom of the hole to keep the sides from falling in. It gave the livestock a place to drink. I watched the pecking order as the animals decided it was time for water. One of the younger cows would head for a drink and soon Agnes would come and run her off, then Joe would run Agnes off, then Tika would run Joe off. When each was satisfied, the sequences reversed, but by the time Agnes left, the tub was empty and Daphne stood guard, waiting for the water to replenish. When she left, the calves alternated, looking for a place to squeeze their nose into the tub. Not much else had been done in the plan.

There was a rumor that the property Thornton was renting for his dairy operation would be repossessed. Osterland, the man who leased it to Thornton, had disappeared, and the Websters held a mortgage. I was a little embarrassed to call Don and ask him about the land because I had not done everything on my own farm plan yet. But I could see that this land did not have any problem with slope. Don said he did not even want to come out and look at it because they were coming out with some new "swampbuster" law, and he would have to determine if it was a wetland before he could even tell me which way the water drained. He added that if it was a wetland and I drained it, he could not help me any more. However, he agreed it was some of the best land in the area.

Chapter Three

Lunch at the Ox Yoke Restaurant

Mary grew up in the house in which we lived and has many fond memories of looking out the window and watching the cattle graze on the valley's lush pastureland. Now from that same window, she saw a notice tacked on a tree. As she focused her field glasses, she called out the window, "Francis, come here and look at this. They've posted a sign that says SHERIFF'S SALE on that property across the street."

Mary thought I was pulling weeds in the garden, and I had been doing exactly that until the man started tacking up the sign. "Yes, I'm just coming back from reading it. The guy who put it up said he was in a hurry but we could call the sheriff's office if we were interested."

"Let's buy it," Mary said quickly.

"We'll check into it," I answered slowly.

As the days passed, we talked more and more about what could be done with the property if someone bought it for some commercial enterprise. Because of the spring floods, about the only place for a building would be on the high ground right across from our window. We envisioned some honky-tonk, with its accompanying night noises, blocking our view of the valley. Certainly the bush with the yellow warblers nest would go to make room for the driveway. If they returned at all, the migrating waterfowl, which included some whistling swans, would be hidden from view.

Mary continued to repeat, "Let's buy it."

I continued to reply, "I'll look into it."

Mary attacked with all her sentimental reasons, such as how much fun it would be to build a bonfire and ice skate on the muck under a full moon with the temperature below zero, or how beautiful it would be with the black and white cows grazing in the vivid green summer pasture. I began to look into it!

I went over and talked with Jim Thornton, and he told me the last two rent checks had gone uncashed. Then he led me out of the barn and said the whole area, from the dike to the corn field and from the railroad tracks to the barn, was where the Websters grew their vegetables.

"What are you going to do when this is sold?" I asked.

"I have a lease until June next year. The new owner will have to honor the lease and after that I may decide to get out of dairying."

"Are you going to bid on it?" I asked.

"No. There's a good chance Lorraine will get it back and then I can rent from her. It's good land, but you would have to clean the ditches to grow crops on the muck, and it might be too wet to get a backhoe in there now."

Later, I put on a pair of hip boots and went for a walk, crisscrossing the field. I had to agree with Jim that there were too many soft spots to drive in with a backhoe. The old ditches were still defined, and I figured I could clean down the middle of them with a hand shovel enough to dry up the area.

Mary and I went to see Mr. Hebe, one of the local attorneys, because we had never been involved with a sheriff's sale before and we did not want any unpleasant surprises to crop up. Mr. Hebe said he would accompany us to the sale and advise us on the legal obligations and deed restrictions.

We arrived at Mr. Hebe's office about fifteen minutes before the sale was to begin. His receptionist punched a button on her phone, informed him that we were there, and suggested we have a seat in the waiting room. We had hardly settled into the chairs when we heard a door close and footsteps in the hall. Mr. Hebe is a big man and timidity is not his most noticeable trait. He started talking even before he came into view.

"We did a title search and that didn't show anything to be concerned about. There are some back taxes you'll have to pick up, and I'll check when we get to the courthouse to see if there were any claims filed since yesterday. Otherwise it all looks okay."

On the way to the courthouse we told him of what we were afraid would happen if we didn't buy the land and that we figured it would be easier farming that land than the side of the hill. We also told him we were willing to pay forty thousand dollars in total expenditures for the clear title.

"If you buy it, then you can control it," Hebe said.

When we arrived at the courthouse, he pointed to the sheriff's office and said, "Go on in and get settled and I'll check for any late-filed claims." Quickly, he headed across the hall.

Mary Lou Hinneman, the secretary for the sheriff, was reading something about what gave the sheriff the authority to sell the property when Mr. Hebe returned, gave us a wink, and held up his fingers in an okay sign.

The attorney for Lorraine Webster said, "We bid $37,715 plus the legal costs and obligations."

I looked at Mr. Hebe. I didn't know how much all those pluses added up to, and I thought it would be rather stupid to put in a bid and then find out I was a few dollars too low.

I turned to the secretary and asked, "Can you calculate that bid?"

She started shuffling through some papers and proclaiming what seemed to be significant numbers. Mr. Hebe leaned over and said, "It's right in the ball park."

I looked at Mary and she whispered, "Save the swans!"

I turned to the secretary and asked, "Is this an auction bid? Does Lorraine have the right to bid again?"

The answer came, "Yes, she does."

I was quiet for a minute, then I said, "I bid $37,725 plus the costs and obligations."

The secretary looked around the room and back to Lorraine. "Do we have another bid?" she asked. "If we don't, then the highest bid is $37,725 plus costs."

Mary Lou turned to me and asked, "How are you going to pay for it?"

"I'll write a check."

"You will be in big trouble if it is not a good check."

"Call the bank and talk to Mr. Wilkenson if you want," I replied.

"That won't be necessary," Mary Lou said, and she began calculating the final amount of the sale.

Lorraine came over and said, "You have some wonderful land there, but you will never get any help draining it."

I was surprised and answered, "For another eleven dollars you could have kept it!"

Back at Mr. Hebe's office, he said, "You got a good farm at a good price."

"I might have left a little on the table, but I'm satisfied," I answered.

Speculation was that if Lorraine got the property back, she would be forced to sell it at a lower price because she couldn't go out and clean the ditches herself. On the way home we stopped and bought a round-point shovel.

For a month or so, I spent several hours a day working with my hand shovel. Then Mary told me about a lunch meeting in Galeton at the Ox Yoke Restaurant. The paper said it was for all people who worked in or near runs or streams, or for those who owned property adjacent to runs or streams. I certainly felt I qualified, and the price was reasonable, so I called for a reservation. I thought the people were getting together to clean out the old flood trash, but it was almost all loggers who attended. Apparently there were some laws requiring permits to cross streams or runs, and some loggers were a little lax in applying for them.

A multimedia presentation was given, showing the good and bad ways of timbering from the Fish Commission's viewpoint. They stressed sedimentation control and not disturbing runs and streams. Sediment was considered a pollutant and polluting streams was a violation.

I found the discussion that followed to be interesting. Of course, because I didn't do any timbering, I was not emotionally involved, but I could see there was a wide range of individual concerns. The proponents wanted everyone to get a permit and to adhere precisely with the sketches and plans on the permit application.

One man representing a large lumber company asked loudly, "You want me to move thirty men and my equipment into a site and then if we can't locate a road where we planned because there is a spring there, you want me to send everyone back home and let my equipment sit for a couple of months until you can revise my permit to go around the spring?"

A small operator who used a horse to drag the timber complained, "I would have to draw a different sketch for every tree I cut!"

This question-and-answer session went on for a while, and it appeared to me that one side was saying they did not care what it cost, they wanted to make life easy for the fish. The other side seemed to be saying that they respected the fish and would do what they could to protect them, but they had to make a living and it didn't make sense to have some guy in Harrisburg or State College make judgments that could be better made by someone on the site. It was apparent the main point of the meeting was to keep any pollutant, which included dirt, out of the streams.

People who had a long drive home began to leave, and the man running the discussion asked if there were any other questions.

A lady spoke up. "I have a creek which flows through my property, and my neighbor won't clean the trash out of his part of the creek. When we have a rain, the water backs up into my yard."

The man on the side of the Fish Commission started in by saying, "Sometimes things can be beneficial in the water. We put old tires in strategic places when we build a dam so the fish will have a place to spawn."

Someone across the room asked, "What about those junk cars in Marsh Creek?"

The Fish man replied, "The Fish Commission didn't put those cars in there and the Fish Commission isn't going to take them out."

That's when I remembered Lorraine saying, *You'll never get any help draining it.*

Chapter Four

Cleaning the Ditches

It doesn't take a lot of concentration to throw shovelful after shovelful of residue up on the ditch berm. As I worked my thoughts wandered. I mused as I recalled looking down from my side hill at the panoramic view of the valley and pondering the land below. As Marsh Creek meanders through the property there is a big bend of about 140 degrees, changing from 135 to 275 on the compass. At that point the general lay of the valley makes a sweeping change from 210 degrees to 275. The land I planned to return to productivity lay east and north of this bend.

The floating sticks and debris marked the lazy current of Marsh Creek. The old network of ditches was defined by the water sitting in them. I could see the dike which outlined the field and the ditches that ran alongside. The opening in the corner of the dike was about thirty yards from the big bend in the creek, and cleaning this thirty yards of outlet ditch would allow the field to begin to drain. I could visualize the flow of water through the spur ditches into the headers, merging at the corner of the dike before passing out to the creek. I didn't need Don Lindsey or anyone else to tell me which way the water would run.

The first thing I did was clean the branches and trash at the mouth of the outlet ditch. Then I worked toward the dike with my round-point shovel, digging about eight inches deep. After progressing about twenty yards, I hit something solid. Probing and digging, I uncovered the remains of an old equipment bridge. Someone had constructed a bridge with old railroad ties, and it remained partially collapsed in the ditch.

As I cleaned out under the ties I pictured in my mind what it must have looked like when this bridge was first used. The mountains in the background were in a state of change. Stands of virgin pine, tamarack, and hemlock remained next to newly timbered areas with nothing more than stumps remaining. There were also areas where nature was already filling back in with shrub growth.

Route 6 had not yet been built, so I had to block out the trailer-trucks with the diesel smoke lingering behind them. There weren't any willow trees along the dike and I pictured the dike doubling as a lane. Then I became more sure of my vision. Instead of canary grass, there were vast fields with row after row of crisp green celery contrasting against the rich black muck upon which it thrived. The ditches, instead of being collapsed and filled with cattails, were weed-free with grass banks, and a pair of mallards basked in the sun. On this very bridge was a horse-drawn cart loaded with wooden crates of celery headed toward the washhouse. I could almost hear the giggles of the two small children seated among the crates, dangling their feet over the side of the cart.

I dug a little sediment pool so silt wouldn't fill back in under the bridge, and I continued on toward the dike. An agricultural tribe of Indians, whose chief's name was Cornplanter, had lived here. The Indians didn't have the land divided into parcels with deeds recorded in the courthouse and they followed nature more than we do. The beavers would build a dam and create a lake, then the sediment would settle onto the lake bed. The beavers would exhaust their food supply of young ash trees and move out. Without the beavers to maintain the dams, the lake would drain, leaving the enriched bed to be planted. The Indians probably used a system like the "chair" system used in Chicago after a big snow. The Chicagoans shovel snow off the public street and put a chair in the clean spot to show it is their parking place.

When I reached the dike, I met with another manmade structure. Digging around a steel plate, I uncovered the remains of a water gate. This gate regulated the level of water allowed to remain in the ditches. It would be closed completely in the rain to protect the field from flooding by the rising of Marsh Creek. It could also be adjusted to retain the water from the spring-fed ditches in dry weather. I was told it had been closed in the winter and the ice from the ditches was harvested and stored under sawdust and hay in the ice house. When they quit harvesting ice the gates were left open and the winter rains would cause Marsh Creek to back up and flood the fields. That is what had frozen and provided the muck ice that was part of my wife's fond memories. Now I understood how they could build bonfires on the ice-skating rink.

For a while after the flood protection dams were built in the fifties it would take an exceptionally hard rain to flood the muck, but now with the trash in the creek it flooded regularly. Before the dams were built, a hard rain would clean out the trash in the creek, which is why, I suppose, hard rains are called gullywashers.

I removed the steel plate that had been the door to the gate, tossed it on top of the dike, and worked to where the main ditches merged. After studying the water flow from the ditches that ran alongside each leg of the dike, I decided to keep going straight along the western part. It was slow going, and every few days I cleaned the sediment from the hole by the bridge.

The roots of the willow trees were a source of irritation. I chopped at them with a grub ax but often I didn't cut them completely, and I ended up twisting and yanking on them to break them off.

One such battle was impeded by a branch that had settled in the ditch. I grabbed the branch and found it was embedded in the silt. I gave a good yank and it broke loose, sending me off-balance backward. I let go of the branch, propelling it over my head as I reached back to support myself with my hand. My feet were mired in the ditch and I couldn't roll out, so I fell back and caught myself with my other hand behind me. There I was with my hands behind me, sinking slowly into the muck. I held my hips as high as I could, and there was about one inch between the seat of my pants and the water in the ditch. I was trying to figure out how to get out of there without sitting in the ditch when I heard a buzzing sound over my head. Suddenly I was ten feet away in the tall canary grass, looking back at the broken wasp nest and trying to figure out how I got there without getting my britches soaked. I took a look at the wasps, decided my shovel would be all right right where it was, and walked back to the house.

The next day the wasp nest was still hanging in the tree. It had a big hole in it and there was a lot of activity around it. After cautiously retrieving my shovel I went back to the outlet ditch. Working a short distance up the main ditch that ran along the southern portion of this field, my shovel hit a solid object. It was a section of clay tile. I marveled at the work and ingenuity that had gone into this farm. They had run tiles from a spring to this ditch and then worked the land right over the spring and tiles.

A couple of days later I again hit something. Thinking it to be another tile, I reached down and grabbed hold of it, but when it moved, I jerked my hand back. I dug around it and then scooped it up. I had a big turtle balanced momentarily on the shovel and then it dropped onto the bank. It took a defensive stance and I thought I would test it. I broke off a small branch from a willow tree and reached the end down toward the turtle. It snapped the end right off. I backed off about three feet and watched it disappear into the soft muck. That was the end of my digging for a week.

I still had a lot of work to do to clean all the ditches, and I went back to it. After progressing about two hundred feet, I came to a side ditch which ran parallel to the ditch with the now-mended wasp nest, and I started up it. In a couple of days I had reached a low-lying area where the ditch swale contained cattails. Preferring not to work in such wet conditions, I went back to the dike and headed east along the main ditch. Two hundred feet later I came across another side ditch and again worked up this ditch until I came to more cattails. Back to the main ditch again, another two hundred feet, and another side ditch with the same results. These cattail areas were where the first of the two original main ditches had been crossed over when the ditches were relocated in 1969. After extending the side ditches through the other original ditch, and after putting spur ditches into the old mains, there were eleven open ends and about twenty-five hundred feet of ditches. I calculated that it had taken me a thousand hours of work to get this far.

I went back to the outlet and studied the water coming from my ditches and that coming down Marsh Creek. I could see the contrast as the two merged. The water from my ditch was clear and that which came down the creek was cloudy. I reached into the creek with a stick, and when I took it out there was a web of slime hanging between the forks of the branch. I washed it off in my ditch and tossed it aside.

The Wellsboro sewer plant had been inadequate for years, and the industrial waste discharged into the creek just added to the mess. I was told that the few (in the valley) had to suffer for the many (in town). I cleaned the sediment pond and called it a day.

When deer season came the canary grass was still so high that the deer could stand up in the field and the hunters still could not see them. I had on my orange hat and vest, but when I saw my neighbor with a rifle in one hand and a nearly empty bottle of beer in the other, I decided to wait until after hunting season to do any more ditch cleaning.

There wasn't very much more to clean in this field, but it was getting colder and I was having more and more muscle cramps. I wanted to be able to work the land in the spring, so I kept at it.

One February morning I was cleaning the barn for Thornton when Jim said enthusiastically, "You should see the little digger John Deere has. They have come out with a backhoe on a turret and tracks."

Without changing the rhythm of my shoveling, I said, "So?"

Jim continued, "It would be just the thing for cleaning ditches."

I replied, "I'm doing all right with..." as I started to lift the shovel laden with manure, my voice became slowed and strained, "...my round-point shovel."

Jim went on, "It does a 360—you could make some pads and walk right across the muck."

I paused before picking up the next shovelful and said, "I will look into it."

I discovered the machine could be rented by the day, so I agreed to rent it for a couple of days to see if it would do what we thought it would do.

Not wanting to get it stuck in a field inaccessible to a tractor, I had them drop it off in the field between Marsh Creek and the barn. There was a long ditch that went from a conduit under Webster Road to where it entered the creek after the creek curved, about six hundred feet downstream. The barnyard had standing water and the low spot in the field was where I planted Jim's manure spreader the first day I cleaned his barn. They used to use dynamite to open this ditch because it went through some deep muck. Every time they tried to clean it with any kind of equipment, they got stuck.

After putting some handles made of cables in each end of two sheets of one-half inch plywood to use as pads, I began working my way up from the creek by moving a pad from where I had been to where I was going, while sitting on the other one. By the time I reached the deep muck I had a pretty good feel of the controls.

The ditch widened and the frosted berm turned into a thin layer of ice over the wet muck. I walked the little John Deere 15 mini-excavator out on the pad and heard the ice crack. Seconds later the plywood cracked, and the little machine began to tilt and sink. By using the shovel to right it, I was able to drive back onto the pad from where I had just come. I went into town, bought four sheets of three-quarter inch plywood, doubled them up, and went right back to digging.

I could see cars stop on Webster Road and their drivers watch as I worked through the soft muck. I wondered what the odds at the barber shop in town were as to whether I would get stuck. I was convinced the system would work, so I called the dealer and told him, "Don't come back to get the digger in the morning. I am going to buy it."

When I neared the road, I dug up a long three-quarter inch pipe with a elbow and an eighteen inch nipple. I wondered how badly clogged the conduit was and if I could open it with this pipe. As I dug out the opening, I was pleased to see water bubbling out. I dug a hole for the stones to drop into, and soon the water was gushing freely.

It was time for lunch, so I parked the digger and walked through the pasture to the pond behind my house. There was a noticeable current as the water was drawn through the tiles leading to the conduit. I built a dam of branches, rocks, and cattails, which slowed the flow enough so the tiles became exposed as the water gurgled and swirled down them. Mary appeared and announced, "You are draining my duck pond."

I told her, "I will dam it up better after lunch. It isn't going to lose that much water." Mary went to prepare lunch and I worked on the dam by putting on a couple of hay bales and some more rocks. There was still a trickle of water seeping through, but I figured if the branches didn't break and the whole thing collapsed the cattails would probably float in and seal it off.

We had not yet moved into that house, but because I was working down there, Mary had come down for lunch. The stump in the pond outside the kitchen window showed that the pond had lost about one inch of water.

The top speed on my digger was one-point-something miles per hour. I debated whether to take it down the road to finish that fifteen acre field or finish it by hand. It would take me half a day to move the machine, but it was easier, faster, and more fun. I used the digger to go over the main ditch again and I went to the end which needed finishing. I didn't need my pads until I got to the far end, where there was a spring.

The big house in the valley had been built by the Websters when they were growing vegetables. Now two generations later, it was no longer in the family. It had been sold along with eleven acres from the farm. Ron Lundgren, a restaurant owner who was connected with Ducks Unlimited, owned it, and then a doctor who worked at the fish hatchery. We purchased it after the doctor was transferred to a new location.

After moving in, we went for a canoe ride on the pond and found it was choked with vegetation. Besides the cattails closing in from the sides, there were weeds dragging under the canoe as we paddled across the more open parts. Mary wanted to raise the dam to make more clearance, but I favored cleaning out some of the weeds. I was going to work on the small third nearest the house and leave the rest untouched. My plan was to scrape the weeds and make a small island with some mud flats, hoping to attract some sandpipers and dowitchers along with a variety of ducks.

After the ducklings were mature, I put a dike across the narrow part and opened the dam. The water this side of the dike drained through the tiles. A couple of duck hunters came by to look for ducks. Two-thirds of the pond still had water in it, but from the right-of-way, it looked all drained. I didn't like so much shooting that close to my house anyway, so I said, "It doesn't look like the duck hunting will be very good this year."

Then I received a notice in my mailbox that there was a certified letter for which I would have to go into town and sign.

Chapter Five

The Registered Letter

I drove into town and signed for the registered letter. It was from the Army Corps of Engineers. I opened it right there in the lobby and read it. It was written on Department of the Army stationery and had the Department of Defense seal in the upper left hand corner.

Nov. 12 1987
Operations Division
Subject: CENAB-OP-RE (Burnier, Francis A.) 88-0242-1

Mr. Francis A. Burnier
R.D. 7
Wellsboro, PA 16901

Dear Mr. Burnier:

A recent field investigation disclosed that you have placed dredged fill material in wetlands adjacent to Marsh Creek as part of a wetlands drainage project at your property in Delmar Township, Tioga County, Pennsylvania.

Records in this office indicate that neither a Department of the Army permit nor a letter of permission authorizing this work was issued by this office. The placement of fill material in waters of the United States or an adjacent wetlands without prior approval of plans by the Department constitutes a violation of Section 404 of the Clean Water Act.

No further work is to be performed at this or any other loca-tion in a waterway or on wetlands without compliance with the law. Violations of Section 404 are subject to prosecu--tion by the Attorney General of the United States. You are to furnish this office within 10 calendar days following receipt of this letter, the name and address of the contrac-tor who performed this work.

If you have any questions concerning this matter, you may contact Mr. Irwin Garskof of this office at (717) 962-2781.

Sincerely,

Thaddeus J. Rugiel
Chief, Enforcement Section

Copy Furnished:

Environmental Protection Agency
Fish and Wildlife Service - State College (w/copy of map)
Pennsylvania Department of Environmental Resources -
Harrisburg
Pennsylvania Fish Commission
Pennsylvania Game Commission

CERTIFIED MAIL
RETURN RECEIPT REQUESTED

My first thought was that some duck hunter who didn't know I was just draining part of my pond temporarily to improve it had made a complaint. I thought of the man who had been dragging a mallard across my front yard when I returned from the barn the first day of duck season. I said hello but he just quickened his pace and avoided me as much as he could. I figured he must have felt a little funny walking past the NO TRESPASSING sign, but I didn't pursue him to see who he was.

I marched out of the post office, jumped into the car, and drove straight home to show Mary the letter. We read it over and over and it just didn't make sense. I called Garskof and at first he did-n't know who I was or what I was talking about. I told him he had the wrong guy if he thought I was the one polluting the water or filling in wetlands. When I asked him why they were getting after me, he got out my file and told me it was for putting dredged fill material in a field behind Jan Terry's house. I got more and more worked up.

"You're telling me I have to get a permit to clean a ditch in my own field?" I shouted.

Garskof replied, "You can't do any work in a wetland without first getting a permit."

"Why did you come after me? Everyone cleans their ditches around here and the rest of them use equipment three times as big as mine."

Mr. Garskof said, "I received a anonymous tip about your project and if there are any other violations reported to me I will enforce them just as aggressively."

I said, "I cleaned those ditches with a hand shovel. This whole farm is full of ditches. How do I know which ones I can clean and which ones I can't?"

He said, "Someone will have to come and look at the land to tell you where you can work and where you can't."

"If I was doing something wrong, why didn't you knock on my door or call me on the phone and tell me, instead of sending me a letter saying the attorney general was going to get me?"

"I followed proper procedure," he replied.

I could see we were not going to get this settled on the phone, so I said, "Look, if you could come out here, I can tell you what I'm doing. You can look at the farm and maybe we can get this straightened out."

"Let me see my schedule...I...I could come on November 24."

I said, "Good."

I took the letter over to the neighbor who did the most digging around there, and he said, "Tell them to shove it up their (deleted)."

I showed Thornton the letter the next morning, and he said, "Someone didn't like you posting your land."

"If Lundgren wanted to keep having duck hunting parties for his political buddies he shouldn't have sold the property in the first place. I can't believe he figures he has the same rights to my property as when he owned it," I quipped.

For the next few days, I didn't sleep much. I showed the letter to neighbors and friends. Everyone seemed to have a different opinion on what had precipitated the letter: I drained Arnold Hayden's duck hunting pond; I was a flatlander; I posted my land; I had adopted a couple of black kids; someone was mad because I bought the land when they could have gotten it cheaper from Mrs. Webster; Jan Terry was mad because I told him if I sold him some land it would carry a restriction on it so he couldn't put up some honky-tonk.

Four names kept coming up: Ron Lundgren and friends because of his association with Ducks Unlimited; John Snyder, the local game protector; Arnold Hayden, the game biologist whose job it was to know where the wild birds and animals were and who claimed the best duck pond in the area was the one behind my house; and my neighbor Jan Terry who, in my belief, lost his license for D.U.I. There were a few who thought Jack Cupper of the Audobon Society and the Pine Creek Headwaters Protection Group were involved. Nobody thought that cleaning my ditches in my canary grass field was the reason for it.

I went into town to the Soil Conservation Office and showed the letter to Norm Johnson, the district manager, but nobody there knew anything about it. Norm said, "We are usually part of a permit process, but nobody contacted us on this." I told him Garskof was coming to my house November 24 and that he was more than welcome to come. Norm said he had a prior commitment but maybe Paul or Ralph could come.

I went for the regular scheduled appointment to see my doctor, and the first thing he said after taking my blood pressure was, "What is bothering you?" I told him about the letter and he gave me the standard prescription, "Try not to let it bother you."

I didn't want to take a chance that my phone call to Garskof went unrecorded, so I mailed off this letter to Rugiel within the ten day period:

Dear Mr. Rugiel,

In response to your letter dated Nov. 12, 1987.

I called Mr. Garskof and he informed me that the alleged violations of Sec. #404 of the Clean Water Act pertained to property behind Jan Terry's house where I opened a ditch.

This property is located downstream from the Wellsboro sewage plant and numerous individual and commercial enterprises. I was more than a little surprised that the Army Corps of Engineers would single me out as being in violation of the Clean Water Act.

When I inquired at a local lab that tests water, I was told that unless I find out what specifically to test for it could cost me $2,000. I don't have a lot of money, but if you could meet me there with a couple of glasses we could fill one from my ditch and one from Marsh Creek and I will drink the one from my ditch.

I did the work myself but it was Agway of East Ave., Wellsboro, who sold me the round-point shovel with the wooden handle.

The U.S. Department of Interior, Fish & Wildlife Service wetland map, Keeneyville Quad. dated 5/83 shows the ditch opened.

Since opening that ditch behind Terry's house I have purchased a small power shovel. I have some knowledge of the "swampbuster" provisions of the Food Security Act of 1985. Perhaps you could inform me as to when compliance with the swampbuster provision is not adequate. I am sure the attorney general of the United States has more important things to do than to prosecute some poor uninformed farmer who doesn't know where he can't clean a ditch.

Francis Burnier

I thought I would call John Snyder and confront him with the issue. His old phone number had been discontinued and information informed me his new number was not listed. I tried calling the Game Commission Office, but their number was not working and information could not supply me with a new number. I never liked doing business with an outfit you couldn't contact by phone, but I hadn't initiated this mess. I did get a phone number for Hayden, but when I called I got a machine, and even though I repeated my number he never called me back. Deer season was coming and I couldn't find any way to get in touch with anyone in the Game Commission.

I vowed to find out who was behind all this and I wrote a letter to be printed in the local paper. Mary read it and didn't like me saying "some spineless two-legged rat," so I changed it to "some individual or group with considerable political influence and lacking in backbone." I talked to Bob Miller, the advertising editor, and told him I wanted to run this letter—along with the one to Rugiel and the one I got from the Corps—where the hunters would see them. Bob sent me back to the newsroom and Terry Miller said he would take care of the notice of violation letter. I went back to Bob and told him I would pay for those two letters, and I gave him a copy of the letter to Rugiel and an open letter to all hunters.

The letter was intended to inform the hunters that my property was no longer open for the general public's use until I found out who had initiated this enforcement action.

I left the *Gazette* office, came home, and called Arnie Borden, the Delmar Township supervisor, and I read the notice of violation to him. Arnie said, "Who's mad at you?" I told him about Terry wanting to buy some of my land to make a dude fishing ranch. Arnie used a lot of adjectives to describe Terry and told me they were having a public meeting that night with the Department of Environmental Resources because Terry had claimed a neighbor had put in a new septic without first getting a permit.

Thornton went with me to the meeting. Three men from the D.E.R. were there and read a list of alleged violations which had occurred in Delmar Township over the last few years. Arnie was a lot cooler than I would have been. He started explaining one by one.

"In that case they moved a trailer house into a place where there had been a trailer before and the septic was already there. In this case the man was cleaning a septic on Friday afternoon when the tank collapsed. Your permit people had left for the weekend and he had to wait until Monday to get the permit. I suppose he could have told them not to take a bath or go to the toilet over the weekend, but since it was a standard installation he put the tank in and got the permit when your office opened. This case I will grant was a violation in that the septic was not up to code, but the lady lives alone, is indigent, and at least she had a pot she could pee in. In this case, I agree again, but I tried to get him to correct the violation. He took it to court and the judge ruled in his favor. I would be in contempt of court if I pressed the issue."

When the spokesman for the D.E.R. started talking again, you could see some of the wind had gone out of his sails, but after a while he was pumped up again. Arnie said, "Yes, it is possible that someone on a back road could put in a septic without me knowing it. I don't have enough manpower to drive every road every day and check every septic."

The D.E.R. man said, "Find some little guy and make a example of him and the rest will fall in line."

I was dumbfounded. The entire evening was spent with D.E.R. and township people arguing petty violations from years ago, all because Jan Terry had suspected his neighbor of a violation, called the D.E.R., and told them the township wasn't doing its job. I left the meeting with the feeling the whole thing would be replayed the next day with the Corps at my house.

Jim was really upset, and all the way home he kept saying, "Find a little guy and make and example of him."

Chapter Six

The Bureaucrats Descend en Masse

November 24, 1987

Ralph Brugger from the Tioga County Conservation District and Paul Schafer of the Soil Conservation Service were the first to arrive. We had not yet decided whether to go into the house or wait outside for Mr. Garskof when Thornton drove up. Ralph and Paul were dressed for the field but Jim and I were dressed for the house. We decided to wait inside. We talked a little about the township meeting and were speculating as to what Mr. Garskof would have to say. Both Paul and Ralph said they were there to learn. Ralph had brought a copy of Webster's old farm plan, and we felt prepared to show Garskof that this was a farm and that I wasn't hurting any wildlife or polluting anything.

They asked me who all was coming, and I told them, "As far as I know it is just Garskof, but as angry as I was on the phone I wouldn't be surprised if he had a police escort." We looked out the window and watched as a parade of cars came into the driveway. Each car had a different insignia on the door, and as the doors opened, out stepped men in different uniforms and civilian dress.

Jim said, "Golly, this is just like the movies," and added, "and we are the ones who are outgunned."

I met them as they came up the steps. Mr. Garskof introduced himself, Hugh Palmer, and Dennis Bernhardy of the Pennsylvania Game Commission, Larry Copenhaver of the Pennsylvania Department of Environmental Resources Bureau of Dams and

Waterways, and Dennis Brown of the U.S. Fish and Wildlife Service. Mr. Garskof said, "We would like to discuss the permit requirements as they relate to work in wetlands, and we would like to conduct a site inspection."

I said, "Fine with me. Do you want to come in first or go for a walk first?"

Irwin looked around and said, "It doesn't matter." There were fewer people dressed for the field than the house, so we decided to come inside first.

Our parlor wallpaper features a border with an artist's conception of waterfowl and plants. Canada geese, bluewinged teal, whistling swans, and sandpipers are among the cattails. All can be seen out our kitchen window on the real pond behind the house. I noticed my wife had selected the latest editions of our nature magazines to leave on the coffee table. We went into the dining room and I purposely sat on the side of the table so Garskof could observe the feeder out the window behind my back. We have a small stand of pine next to our house and we have pretty good luck attracting birds to our feeders.

Mr. Garskof started in. "Just for a little history of what brings us here, let me give you a brief resume. In 1899 the Rivers and Harbors Act was passed, which required any filling, dredging, or obstructions of navigable waters to be permitted by the Corps of Engineers. The clear intention of the Act was to protect the waters used for commercial navigation. In 1968 the Corps rewrote its permit regulations to include not only the effect on navigation but also the impact on fish, wildlife, conservation, pollution, aesthetics, ecology, and the general public interest. In 1972 the Congress extended the Corps' regulatory jurisdiction to include all waters of the United States, including wetlands. Since 1977 the Corps' wetland policy is that no alteration of wetlands takes place unless it is demonstrated as being in the public interest. In making these decisions, the Corps relies on the views of the Fish and Wildlife Service and the Environmental Protection Agency."

He started to lose me but I got the picture that a law that was written to protect the shipping industry in the major rivers was being used to protect the frogs and birds in any place that ever got wet. Then he started to get a little more personal.

"On October 26 we held a on-site inspection of your property and found—"

I cut him off. "Who do you mean we?"

"There was Norma Kline from the E.P.A., Larry, Dennis, and myself."

"Come on now, think. Wasn't there someone else with you?"

Garskof paused and then said, "Jan Terry."

He went on describing my land with many technical terms and said, "We observed some ditching which caused the draining of wetlands. The land had been flooded in the thirties and has been wetlands ever since."

I interrupted again but with a more relaxed tone in my voice. "From whom did you get your information? Jan Terry?"

Irwin replied, "Some of it came from Terry and others, besides what I observed on my own."

Mary had been in the kitchen listening to everything and I called to her. "Mary, would you come in here and tell Mr. Garskof what you know about this land?"

Mary has a much more pleasing voice than I do, and she began, "I can't tell you about the thirties because I am not that old, but in the forties and fifties I lived in the house across the highway from those fields. Regardless of what Mr. Terry may have told you, those fields were farmed then. In fact, I helped my father harvest the hay off of those fields."

Undaunted, Garskof continued, "What we have here is a valuable ecological system that has been altered."

Everyone started having little side discussions. What was the condition of the land two years ago? Ten years ago. Twenty, thirty, fifty, one hundred. Did its wetland status change back and forth with the conditions? What are wetlands? What is good about them? What is bad? What are good farm practices? What are bad? What is polluted? What caused it? What killed the muskrats? The birds? What attracted the ducks? How much harm do the beavers do? The sewer plant, Marsh Creek, hunters, farmers, townspeople, industry landowners, politicians, environmentalists....

I looked at Garskof, who had stopped talking and was just sitting back in his chair with his eyes shifting to whichever argument seemed to hold the most interest. He seemed content to let the emotions run their course. After a while he resumed control and continued from where he had stopped, "It needs to be restored for the public benefit."

I had a little bit of trouble understanding how it was that I could not farm my land because of its public value. I thought it was bad enough that the fat hunters carried wire cutters so they wouldn't have to climb through the fences, but to keep me from growing feed for my cattle so some guy could shoot a duck seemed a bit too much.

Dennis Brown said something about destroying waterfowl habitat and Mary uncharacteristically spoke up, "Are you familiar with the sora and the rail?"

I looked at Dennis. The U.S. Fish and Wildlife emblem remained upright and formed as the rest of his jacket retreated with his chest as he exhaled and nodded his head. Mary doesn't go around putting people down and I was surprised at her frankness, but she wasn't through. "If we are destroying their habitat, why do they both nest here, along with the hooded merganser, Canada goose, wood duck, and mallard? All raise their young on the pond behind the house."

I was amused and awaited his response, but Mr. Garskof looked at me and said, "This is an important flood plain."

Without a second of hesitation, I replied with a caustic outburst, "So where can you put more water: in a full bucket or an empty one?

Apparently Garskof didn't think my question needed answering any more than my wife's, because he stood up and said, "We had better take a look at the site and we can come back and make recommendations later."

People were putting on boots, zipping up jackets, and getting cameras as I led the way down the hill toward the place where the tiles entered the pond. I didn't announce it as a camera stop, but as I told them how it started draining when I opened the sluice by Webster Road, how I dammed it up until the ducklings matured and then opened it to get at the weeds, there was a steady clicking of shutters.

We walked across the pasture toward the field where I had cleaned the ditches, and every time we passed a low spot with some sedges the cameras would click again. We arrived at the creek and walked across the railroad rails that served as a bridge. The planking had all been washed away in a flood, so all that was left were the bare rails. You could see the outlet ditch from the bridge, and those who felt sure of foot started clicking their cameras again. The others seemed happy to get across without falling in. I hoped the contrast between the creek and my ditch would show up on the film.

We crisscrossed the field, and I showed them—which ditches I used the John Deere and which ones I cleaned by hand. Mr. Garskof seemed puzzled and asked, "Isn't there another ditch that empties into Marsh Creek somewhere?"

I had forgotten about the property line ditch. When the beavers had Marsh Creek dammed up and the water backed up Webster's ditch and flowed down over my land, I had cleaned the ditch between our properties. I said, "There is a common property line ditch, but that isn't worth the walk."

Garskof said, "I would like to see it if it isn't too much trouble."

We headed toward the dry ditch and I thought, *How did they find it the first time?* Terry must have taken them on a very extensive tour of my property. I thought it a waste of time, but Garskof looked at a bend in the creek and wrote some notes.

We headed back to the house, and I asked, "Now that you have seen it, what have I done that is so bad?"

Irwin said, "I have seen worse, but you altered a wetland and you will have to restore it."

I couldn't believe this. The area between the dike and the creek I hadn't drained at all. The property line ditch had no function with the beaver dam gone.

We climbed over a cattle fence and I asked, "What do you want me to restore it to? Like it was when my wife hayed it here? Like it was when they grew celery here? Like it was when Chief Cornplanter roamed these lands? What?"

He said, "You will have to plug up the ditches."

Back at the house they said it was for the public interest, and I said, "You mean so Hayden and friends can shoot ducks."

Mary asked, "Why didn't you buy the land if it is so important?"

They replied, "We would like to, but it would cost too much to buy all the wetlands."

To which Mary responded, "When I don't have enough money to buy something, I either do without or sell something to get the money."

I told Dennis Bernhardy about trying to call Snyder, Hayden, and the Game Commission. He acted as if he did not believe me. I said, "My phone is right here. You try it and see if you have any better luck."

He got the same results I had, and he got into his car and drove off, kicking up stones all the way to the bridge.

About half an hour later, Jim called and asked if I had seen the paper. I said, "I get my paper in the mail tomorrow. Why?"

"My wife wanted to know where I had been today because she read all about it in the paper and they never mentioned my name. But everything is all right because I knew enough about what was said to convince her I was there. It sure is funny that Betty read about it in the paper before it even happened."

The paper had a picture of Garskof and Bernhardy taking a soil sample in one of my ditches with an article explaining that I had come from Chicago and was unlawfully placing fill material in wetlands. I told Mary, "That picture had to have been taken October 26. You sure would have thought in a month's time that the paper could have called to verify the story they were preparing. For that matter, they could have told me they had a story written about me when I paid to have the letter to the hunters printed."

I scanned through the paper and tucked away in the ad section in small print were my letters to the hunters and Rugiel.

Mary, who always advised, "Don't say anything to anyone," sat down and wrote a letter to the editor denouncing the Corps' tactics.

A week later I got a letter from the E.P.A. "I can't believe these people," I said loud enough for the cows in the barn to hear, "Now they want fifty thousand dollars a day for every day the ditches are open. Apparently they want me to restore the integrity of Marsh Creek."

I went into town in search of Bailey Laboratories. I told Mr. Bailey, "I don't want to spend a fortune, but I want some tests made to show it isn't me polluting the creek. I want you to take samples in case this ever goes to court."

Mr. Bailey said, "You may be overreacting a little."

I handed him the letter and said, "Read this."

He read it and agreed, "This isn't exactly pocket change they are talking about. I can take a couple of samples and run some tests for under one hundred dollars."

We set a time to gather the samples and I drove back home.

Norm Johnson called and asked if I could come to a conservation meeting December 11 and tell my story.

Chapter Seven

Soil Conservation Meeting

December 11, 1987

When Norm Johnson asked me to explain how I felt about what had happened regarding the registered letter and the meeting at my house I gave this analogy: Imagine you are driving along rural Route 6 and eating an apple. You get down to the core and contemplate tossing it out the window. You know there is a law against littering that carries a fine. You also know that mice, moles, ants, birds, rabbits, and other creatures will likely consume the core within hours. You have been driving mile after mile without giving the trash along the road a thought. You don't drink, you don't smoke, and when you eat McDonald's, you eat at the store and put your trash in the receptacle. The apple core you are holding between your thumb and forefinger cracks and the palm of your hand becomes moistened as you clasp the broken parts. Now each beer can, each cigarette package, and each Big Mac box you have passed since leaving town returns to your memory. The debate as to whether you would be feeding the wildlife or littering no longer needs to be resolved. You toss the core into the tall grass along the road.

A loudspeaker comes on and you hear a booming voice instructing you to pull it over. A look in your rearview mirror reveals a car with its lights flashing behind you. As you pull over, you watch as a rotating red light is placed on the dash. You almost utter some profanities, thinking you will probably get fined for littering when it could be argued you were only feeding the birds.

The officer puts on his hat, strolls up to the window and asks, "Do you know what you just did?"

You answer, "Yes, I tossed a apple core into the weeds beside the road."

"Well, let me tell you why you are being arrested. We have had some problems with hoodlums throwing brickbats off the bridges into expressway traffic. It happened in Chicago and it happened in California. We have to stop it before it spreads to Pittsburgh or Philadelphia. Now we have this law that prohibits propelling an object onto a public right of way. Lock your car. You will have to come with me and post a fifty-thousand dollar bond."

I told those at the meeting that all I did was clean a ditch in my field with a round-point shovel, I didn't stop the traffic on the St. Lawrence Seaway.

Almost everyone wanted to know who was mad at me. It was pretty obvious that the anonymous "tipster" had influenced the Corps' action. A certain person who wishes to remain anonymous said, "I believe Arnold Hayden is the nigger in the woodpile." When you think of the method of surveillance used by slave owners, his comment was descriptive of what he meant even if it is not in good taste in today's lexicon.

The only one who thought wetland legislation might have had something to do with it was Don Lindsey. Don said, "You might have to apply for a permit."

I replied, "For what do I apply? For what I have already done? What I intend to do? What I would like to do if I had more time and money?" Don just shrugged his shoulders.

Ralph Brugger and Norm Johnson were reading from the Federal Register and citing this regulation and that exception when I asked, "Who knows about these 404 regulations? Mrs. Webster didn't say anything when I bought the property. The banker didn't say anything when he approved the check. The lawyer didn't say anything when he researched the deed. The sheriff didn't say anything at the sale and all you people told me was that if it was a wetland you couldn't help me drain it."

I told them how Garskof started out saying if it had not been farmed for fifty years it could no longer be farmed. After my wife told him she had worked with her father on the land, he said twenty years, and finally, after he found out it was cropped in 1978, he changed his requirements to "if it had not been plowed three of the last five years."

No one seemed to know what regulations applied to whom or when. Don said we needed to get some answers and suggested they hold a meeting with the people who were supposed to know.

Norm sent me a copy of the notes from the meeting and told me Bill Adams from the Pennsylvania Farmers Association was setting up a meeting with the Corps of Engineers, and he asked if I would like to attend. I told him I would be delighted to attend and that I had just received a Notice of Violation from the Pennsylvania Department of Environmental Resources saying that I had drained over one hundred acres of wetland by opening my existing ditches. Norm said, "Oh my, that much? Did they really say one hundred acres?"

Norm didn't know what the Dam Safety and Encroachments Act of November 26, 1978, P.L. 1375, No 325, as amended 32 P.S. 683.6 and 693.18 said, so I went to the courthouse library and got some help. There I read, "693.6 (a) No person shall construct, operate, maintain, modify, enlarge, or abandon any dam, water obstruction or encroachment without the prior written permit of the Department." Since the farm had a lot of ditches and drains that had been installed, relocated, and cleaned, both by hand and machinery of various sizes over the last century and a half, I tried to find out how to walk the line between "maintaining" and "abandoning." I assumed that cleaning the ditches was "maintaining," but I was fearful that not cleaning would be "abandoning."

Bill Adams sent me a copy of the notice of the meeting scheduled for January 25, 1988, and I wrote to Mr. Copenhaver on the nineteenth and told him I hoped some progress could be made at the meeting to resolve any conflict.

I had a lot of questions. I had started cleaning the ditches the day I bought the farm, and I wanted to know when it stopped being a farm and became valuable wetlands which had to be protected for the public good. Was it when I started cleaning the ditches or after I finished? Was it before I bought the land and I, along with the lawyer, banker, sheriff, and widow, just thought it was a farm?

It didn't seem right to me that if you sold a farm on contract and the buyer disappeared without paying, what you got back was no longer a farm. And it didn't seem right that just because Mr. Webster had a stroke and didn't clean the ditches before he died, it couldn't be sold as a farm.

Then Norm called and told me the meeting was canceled. The Corps had backed out of the public meeting in Wellsboro but recommended a private meeting in Harrisburg on the twenty-eighth. I told Norm I would go to Harrisburg to get this straightened out, but he said I wasn't invited. I was disappointed I couldn't sit in on the plans for my own lynching, but Norm said they thought they could get more done that way.

After dropping my daughter off at the Buffalo airport, we were caught in a ferocious snowstorm on the way home. We were driving on a divided, limited-access highway and wondered if it was safe to continue. The fast lane was not being used at all and the slow lane had only a set of tire tracks to follow. I could occasionally make out a set of taillights in front of me. Something fluttered in the snow and Mary and I blurted out simultaneously, "That's a loon."

A loon had been grounded and was flopping in the snow right in the middle of the fast lane. At first I thought the car in front of me had hit him, but as I watched in my rearview mirror as he tried to get airborne I could tell he was not hurt badly. I watched him struggle for a while and said, more to myself than to Mary, "He can't get airborne without some water."

I took my foot off the accelerator and the car slowed so quickly I feared I was stuck. I wasn't going to pull out of the ruts and I didn't want to leave the car in the road and walk back, so I told Mary, "You watch for headlights and I'll try to back up to it if no cars come."

I remembered the black eyes and swollen face of the bulldozer operator at the dump back in Chicago who felt sorry for an injured little green heron and who got his nose broken when he went to move it to the side. I dropped my coat over the loon, picked him up inside the coat, and put him in the back seat. No cars had come and when I learned the road was officially closed I figured I must have been the last one on it.

We drove along and talked about what we should do with the loon. We had a cottage in northern Wisconsin, and there were loons on Lake Nancy. The people were very protective of them, and I said, "With my luck, we will get in trouble for having an endangered species in captivity."

Mary said, "He will die if you turn him loose."

We spotted a New York State trooper and flagged him down. As I approached his car, he was on the radio reading my license number. I motioned for him to roll his window down a little and he obliged. I started out by saying, "I found a common loon in the snow about half an hour ago and I don't know what to do with him." I got a quizzical look and with the snow blowing in his window I figured I had better explain some more. "This loon was laying beside the road and I picked him up. I would take him home with me but I don't want to get in trouble." I could tell I wasn't communicating, so I tried again. "I have this loon in the back seat of my car, and unless you know of a lake nearby with some open water, I will take him home and find a lake tomorrow, in which to put him. I just don't want to get in trouble."

My coat was still in the back seat with the loon, and the wind was blowing up my shirt. I said, "Come and look in the back seat of my car," and I went to get my coat. I saw the trooper had picked up the mike for his radio, and then it came to me that this trooper did not know there was a bird called a loon. I put my coat on and took my time to explain that what I had in my car was a bird that needed to have some water in order to get airborne.

The trooper seemed to relax a little. He opened the car door, got out, and peered into my car. He told me to come with him to his car and he would call on the radio for instructions. In a very professional tone he explained, "The subject has a loon in his car and awaits instruction as to the proper dispatching of same." The operator said he would call someone from the Conservation Service and get back to him. After a couple of minutes the word came that I should put the bird in some water and it would be fine. The trooper turned to me and said, "There is a small sanitation stream in town where the water hardly ever freezes."

I didn't even wait for instructions on how to find the stream. "Thanks, but I will find a lake for him tomorrow. I just don't want to get in trouble for having him in captivity."

Chapter Eight

To Plug or Not to Plug

Mary and I began to polarize on what to do. I wanted to tell them to take me to court if they thought I was doing something wrong, and Mary wanted me to apply for a permit. It didn't make sense to me to plug up the ditches in order to apply for a permit to clean them. The parts of the one thousand or so hours I had spent cleaning the ditches that came to mind now were the cold, miserable ones. Mary said, "You enjoyed cleaning the ditches and watching the field dry up so you could harvest the hay." But even if I had "enjoyed" viewing the results of my labor, all I could think of now were the spider bites, the muscle cramps, and the numb fingers and toes. Mary continued, "You cleaned them once, you can clean them again."

Filling in the ditches and starting over again didn't have much of an appeal, and I asked Mary, "Now that our sixth child is graduating from high school, do you want to go back to having three under three?"

Mary didn't answer my question, but replied, "Garskof told us at the first meeting that it had gone to the Supreme Court and that we had no chance of winning in a court battle."

Somehow I did not believe I was the environmental criminal the paper described. The town sewage floated down through my property. The railroad dumped antifreeze into my pond. The Pennsylvania Department of Transportation shoveled the salt off the bridges into the runs on my property. And when the diesel truck rolled over into my alfalfa field, they took great pains to use kitty litter to pick up the little bit of fuel spilled on the road and ignored the 100 gallons or so that drained onto my field.

The results came from Bailey's lab and showed that the concentration of what the lab called fecal coliform was 4580#/100 coming down the creek as compared to 20#/100 coming out of my ditch. Translated into layman's terms, that meant each gallon of water coming down the creek contained 229 times as much poop as that which came from my property. The more I thought of them coming after me with the Clean Water Act, the angrier I got. I could not sleep, so I got out of bed at one o'clock in the morning and went for a walk.

There was a light cover of snow in the fields, and with the moon shining brightly I was amazed at how well I could see. Everywhere I went I saw wetlands. Some had been cropped this year and some had not. Some had perforated pipes discharging a slow trickle of water into the ditches by the road. Some had shallow open drains with ice forming on the low-lying grass. Barnyards contained bull-dozers, backhoes, and rolls of perforated pipe.

The stars in all their splendor, the sparkle of the moonlit snow, and the crispness of the early morning air could not overcome the anguish in me, and as I walked through the pass on Wolf Run at three o'clock in the morning with ice hanging on my beard, my voice echoed in the hills, "Why me?"

Mary wanted to know where I had been. I told her I had walked Route 6 around the hill and then the back roads over the hill to get back home. I said, "It sure is easy to see why there is always snow up on the Wolf Run pass. When I got there I had to pull my hat down over my ears and button my coat."

Mary didn't like me talking about the Corps and wetlands but I started in anyway. "I did not do anything to harm the environment. Everyone digs and drains. I think we should tell them to take us to court. First they have to prove we did something to harm someone. If they claim some vague benefit to the public, I'll claim they are being arbitrary and capricious in applying the law to us and not to anyone else."

"They will just fine us fifty thousand dollars a day, take everything we have, and put us in jail."

"They won't put *you* in jail."

"I don't want you to go to jail, either."

Frankly I was getting to the place where I didn't much care. I was tired of getting pushed around and I felt like pushing back. I remembered reading about people who sued for the lack of affection they suffered when their spouse had been upset by something. At the time, I thought the huge settlements they got were ridiculous, but now it didn't seem so funny. Mary wanted to do whatever they said, and I wanted to find out what they were really after. I remembered Garskof telling us they would like to buy the wetlands but didn't have enough money, and Mary telling him that when she doesn't have enough money to buy everything, she buys what she can and leaves the rest on the shelf. I agreed with Mary on that. Actually, we agree on a lot of things. We are both concerned with the environment and believe that as much as possible, we should work in harmony with nature. Where I had a problem with this was that they were taking an unjust law and using it vindictively. I told Mary I wanted to find out who was after me and why.

The weather forecast called for a cold spell and I knew the ground would be frozen hard enough to make work difficult. I also knew that if I waited until spring to apply for a permit it would kill another year's harvest. I called Garskof and said, "I have not received the letter from the Corps telling me how to plug the ditches."

He informed me, "I have forwarded my recommendations to Baltimore and you should get a restoration letter in a couple of weeks."

I replied, "If I am going to apply for a permit I need to start now because of the frost."

He said, "I specified a dirt plug thirty inches deep and twenty-five feet long with rocks at the upper end. You could install it before you get the letter if you want."

"I thought sediment was a pollutant, and now you want me to shovel twenty-five yards of dirt into a ditch," I said in disbelief. "Wouldn't it be better to plug it with hay bales and rocks?"

Garskof replied, "You could utilize some bales and rocks for a temporary plug, but you must cover it with dirt, and if your permit is denied you will have to remake it permanently with dirt."

The "if your permit is denied" contrasted with Mary's firm belief that if I went through all the paperwork I would be able to use my field.

Finally I said, "Okay I'll jump through your hoops. I will plug the ditches and apply for a permit and we will see where it gets us."

I loaded the manure spreader with hay bales and rocks, put the round-point shovel and a pickax on top, and went to the area to be plugged. I stopped by the bridge and picked up some picket fence slats and some shelving from the flood trash.

After placing a piece of shelving across the ditch, I drove the fence slats behind it for support and put a bale of hay against it. I jumped on the hay to force it down into the bottom of the ditch. Satisfied with the way it fit, I continued laying hay bales in the ditch until I had the twenty-five feet in length. By this time the water had already begun to rise. I quickened my pace to get another layer of hay bales on before the bottom layer started to float, then I put a big rock on each bale for weight. I broke a bale open, spread it in front of the last bale, and piled rocks on it. There was one bale remaining, so I broke that open and stuffed handfuls of hay in any crack I could find.

All that remained was to cover it with six or eight inches of dirt. Once I had opened up the side of the old dike with the pickax, the rest was dry, or at least not frozen, and I began shoveling dirt on the rocks and loose hay at the front of the plug. The dike was made of muck, and as it hit the water, it dissolved. It seemed senseless to me to cover these bales with eight inches of muck and let it all wash into the creek, so I figured I must not have understood on which end I was supposed to put the rocks. I had not used all the rocks in the spreader yet, so I placed them on the downward end to act as a sediment trap. After topping the plug off with the dirt, I was still uncomfortable with the chances of the muck washing downstream. There were no more rocks in the spreader and the only rocks not covered with dirt were the ones at the front end, under the icy water. I took off my jacket, rolled up my shirt sleeve, fished out six or seven nice-sized rocks, and placed them to raise the height of the sediment trap another two inches. Standing with my numb hands under my shirt halfway to my arm pits, I concluded that the plug would be effective even if it didn't meet with Garskof's approval.

A month later I received the "restoration" letter. The only difference in the plug was that I had put rocks at both ends and used hay bales under the dirt.

I dialed the phone. "Army Corps of Engineers, Garskof speaking."

"Burnier in Wellsboro. I got your letter today and I want to tell you the plug is in place, meets the specifications, and the water has already come up to level. I am ready to start the permit process."

"Er...ah... I will have to come and inspect it before you can begin the permit process."

"I want to open it up early enough in the spring so I don't lose another growing season."

"I will set up a date to inspect it as soon as I can."

It was February 9 when Paul Schafer of the S.C.S. and Ralph Brugger and Norm Johnson of the Tioga County Conservation District (who I had invited) met at my house with Dennis Brown of the United States Fish and Wildlife Service, Dennis Bernhardy and Hugh Palmer of the Pennsylvania Game Commission, Larry Copenhaver of the D.E.R., and Garskof and two other men from the Army Corps of Engineers. The first item on the agenda was to inspect the plugs. We took the stroll from my house through the pasture and over the rails that spanned Marsh Creek.

It had rained before turning cold, and ice covered the plug and the ditches above it. Garskof broke a small branch off a willow tree and trimmed it into a stick about three and a half feet long. "Where does the plug end?" he asked.

Squatting on one leg on the ditch bank, I kicked a hole in the ice with the heel of my foot. We exchanged places and Irwin inserted the stick into the hole. It went down about ten inches and stopped abruptly. He made a couple more thrusts and had the same results. I could hear murmuring in the wolf pack when Mr. Garskof rose, turned, and ceremoniously placed his thumb at the water mark a scant two inches from the end of the stick. He gave me a quizzical look, but in contrast to the New York trooper's look, which had pleaded for a explanation of the loon, this look demanded an explanation of the 2-inch water mark. Before he could say anything, I was around him kicking another hole a foot from the first one. This time the stick went down until his wrist hit the ice. He pushed the stick down, released it, and grabbed it closer to the end. Again his wrist hit the ice, and again he grabbed it higher. The result was the same, and Garskof rose and took hold of the very end of the stick. It wasn't until his hand started to disappear below the ice that the stick came to rest. He rose and set the end of the stick on the ground, but he didn't bother to place his thumb on the water mark. He took one glance and tossed it into the ditch below the plug. Nobody asked, so I did not tell anyone about the railroad ties which had been part of the old equipment bridge. I picked the stick out of the ditch and we all headed back to the house.

Larry Copenhaver and Dennis Bernhardy were walking together, and I thought about the questions I would ask them. I wanted to know if Dennis had talked to John Snyder and Arnie Hayden, and I wanted to hear Larry's explanation as to which ditches were to be maintained and which were to be abandoned.

As we assembled in the dining room I looked for Dennis. Thinking he might be more inclined to talk about Hayden and Snyder in the foyer, I was pleased to see he had not yet joined the group. I returned to the foyer but found no one. I looked out the window and watched Dennis and Larry drive off. Back in the dining room I said, "I wanted to find out how this all came about and what I could and could not do, and the guys with the answers just left."

"Garskof had some pictures that apparently had been provided by Jan Terry, and he proceeded to circulate them as evidence as to the prior wet conditions of the site. There were pictures of the site with a Canada goose on it. There were also some pictures of muskrat houses, but there was no identifying landmark and I never did find out where they were.

"Mary," I called to the kitchen, "bring me those pictures we just had developed."

The first two pictures were shots of me in front of the house holding the loon we had rescued in New York state. The next three were of the loon bring released in Cayuga Lake. They brought a smile to my face as I recalled how the loon swam out underwater for about seventy-five yards, surfaced, and yodeled back at us before swimming out into the lake. There were two pictures of the red streaks in the snow where Conrail had dumped three hundred gallons of antifreeze along the pond behind my house. The rest were all pictures I had taken after the rain and before it froze; my pasture, my barnyard, the neighbor's front yard, and of course the "site," which was the focus of all this nonsense. I handed them to Garskof and asked, "Which of these are wetlands?"

He looked through them and said, "They all are."

As the meeting progressed, they told me I could use some of my land for farming if I would enhance some of the rest for wetlands. I guess I wasn't in much of a mood to give them half of the farm to make up for what I did when I couldn't find out if what I had done was wrong.

"Look," I said, "in addition to the fifty acres of this farm which has already been set aside for wildlife, I have no foreseeable plans to drain and farm most of the vegetable fields you tell me are now considered wetlands."

The reply was, "That is good that you don't intend to drain any more of your fields, because we wouldn't permit it. But that doesn't diminish your need to convert some non-wetlands to wetlands if you want a permit for what you did."

I said, "I can't believe it. You are telling me that most of my land is high-quality wetland that has to be preserved for the good of the public, but even then I can't use this canary grass field unless I enhance something else."

They told me, "We will send someone out to tell you how to enhance your land."

February 18 Paul Schafer, Ralph Brugger, and I took Barry Isaacs, the soil conservation biologist, on the same standard tour of my property. Back in the house we talked about the water fowl we had nesting on our land. Barry wasn't familiar with the hooded merganser and said he would have to do some research to tell us how to enhance its habitat. He talked about clearing seven-foot wide paths through the weeds that were taking over our pond. He told us to expect a lengthy mitigation process once we applied for a permit and that he would prepare a letter of enhancement recommendation. I had heard about neighbors who had received assistance for enhancing land for wildlife use, and I wondered what kind of equipment they had available. Barry told me I would have to provide all the equipment, labor, and money, but they would tell me what would be acceptable to them.

A day or so later I asked Ralph if he would help me with some of the technical aspects of the permit process so I could get the ball rolling.

Chapter Nine

Applying for a Permit

Ralph went to a file cabinet and got out an old copy of Webster's farm plan. It had been prepared in 1948 and updated in 1959 and 1962. It contained a photo map of the farm and showed how each field was used over the years. Then he went to another cabinet and took out a large topographical map of the whole area and spread it on the desk.

"Now, what do you want to apply for a permit to do?" he asked.

"Well," I began, "I would like to clean some of my ditches so I could use part of my land."

"We will have to be a little more specific than that. What is it exactly that you want to do? Look at the fields on this farm plan and tell me which ones you want to work on."

"Well originally I was going to just clean the field that I cleaned because I would have to open a ditch on Mike Hawk's land to drain any more. When Mike told me I could drain through him and get the hay off his land for five years if I did, then I thought maybe I would open this up to Wolf Run. Actually, Wolf Run dissipates when it reaches the flat and needs to be opened up to Marsh Creek."

Ralph started placing his thumb on the map in various positions and covered the map to the top of both hills along Wolf Run. Ralph looked up and said, "Wolf Run has a watershed over three hundred acres, so you would need a permit to open it up."

"Would I get the permit or would Mike?"

"It is the owner's responsibility to get the permit, and that would complicate things."

I sighed and remarked, "That puts us back to what I have already done."

Ralph got out an application booklet which had what I thought was a picture of the Boulder Dam on it, and he started reading.

"All projects require three sets of plans. Okay. Names, addresses, and telephone numbers of all adjacent property owners." Ralph looked at me and said, "You can get that at the tax assessment office," and continued reading. "Identify type of activity. Check the box that best describes your project: culverts and bridges; stream enclosures; channel changes and dredging; fills, levees, floodwall and streambank retaining devices; stream crossing, outfalls and headwalls; docks, wharves and bulkheads; commercial dredging; discharges of dredged or fill material."

I had gone over this form before coming in for help and I couldn't figure out which box to check. I was not going to use any fill, and according to my dictionary, a dredge is a powerful machine equipped with scooping or suction devices used in deepening harbors and rivers. I didn't think of me and my round-point shovel as being a dredge and apparently Ralph didn't either because he dropped his pencil and said, "There is nothing here that covers cleaning existing drains."

Howard Rutledge was listening at his desk and advised us, "Make another box and label it clean existing drains."

When we finished reviewing the form, Ralph said he would make up a soil erosion and sedimentation control plan, and I headed for the courthouse to get the names, addresses, and phone numbers of the adjoining property owners.

Back at the S.C.S. office, we assembled the forms, maps, and sketches that Ralph had prepared for me. I took the erosion and sedimentation plan next door to have the district manager sign his approval. It had been filled out on a standard form on which they explained what could cause erosion and how to minimize it. We went over the checklist and Ralph said, "All that is missing is the proof of notification to Delmar Township and Tioga County."

I jumped into my car and headed for Stony Fork. Shirley Borden was the Delmar Township secretary, and I told her what I needed. She swiveled in her chair and inserted a piece of paper printed with the Township logo into the typewriter along with a carbon and an onion skin. She played a tune on the keys, and in less than a minute she handed me a letter and said, "This should do it."

Before I could move or say thank you she had taken the scribbled letter from my hand, put a paper clip on it and the onion skin copy, and deposited them in a tray on her desk. I still hadn't moved, and Shirley said, "Do you need a envelope?"

I stuttered, "No...no, this is fine," and headed out the door, thinking, *Just one more letter like this.*

The receptionist at the Tioga County Commissioner's office listened to my story in bits and pieces as she operated the phone switchboard. It came as no surprise when she said, "Go around this counter, through this door, and to the right at the end of this next room. You will find Roxie, the commissioner's secretary. Perhaps she can help you."

I told Roxie the same thing I had told Shirley, but instead of igniting a whirlwind of action, Roxie replied, "The planning commissioner isn't here. You will have to come back tomorrow."

"I don't have to talk to the planning commissioner, all I need is a note saying you got this letter." I was pleading. "Who opens the mail that comes here?"

"I do, but I don't write letters unless I'm told," she replied.

I read from Shirley's letter. "This is to advise that the township has received your letter—" and asked, "Can you say that much?"

Roxie persisted, "I have already told you I can't help you. Come back tomorrow."

"Well, I have trouble believing there isn't someone in this office who can acknowledge the receipt of a letter." I guess my voice showed signs of abrasiveness. Roxie went into another office and returned with Commissioner Brian Edgcomb. I explained my plight once again, hoping he would have the authority to acknowledge my letter.

Brian said, "I don't know anything about those permits; that is the planning commissioner's department and you will just have to come back when the planning commissioner is here."

This was the last item I needed to mail off the permit and I couldn't get it. Then I realized my stupidity. There were two acceptable forms of evidence of notification—one was a written acknowledgement, but the other was a certified mail receipt with a copy of the letter sent. "Forget it," I said, "just give me a mailing address for whoever you want to get this and I will mail it."

Roxie wrote: Tioga County Planning Commissioner, 118 Main St., Wellsboro, PA, on a pad of paper, then she tore it off and handed it to me.

I went to the post office, put a quarter in the copy machine, bought a stamp and envelope, paid to have it certified, and came away with change from two dollars and a receipt for the letter. I went back to the copy machine. By placing the receipt on the bottom of the letter, I saved a quarter by coping both at once.

Back at the S.C.S. office, we added the letters to the permit package and sealed the pouch. Back at the post office, I got some change from a five dollar bill for the postage. I took a deep breath and exhaled. This was more frustrating than putting the plug in the ditch and made just about as much sense.

Two weeks later I received in the mail from D.E.R. a form letter that said, "Your application for a permit is incomplete and cannot be processed because ..." and then listed a page of reasons. There were two items checked—"Letter of approval of the Erosion and Sedimentation Control Plan by the district manager" was one. This was remedied when Norman copied word for word onto a paper with the Conservation District logo what was on the form he had signed for the permit application. The other one was "notification of County Commissioner." This had a handwritten explanation. "You must notify the county commissioner, not the planning commissioner."

The form letter went on to say that processing would not begin until the application was complete. There was no signature or indication of to whom to respond.

I wrote a letter to Brian Edgecomb the Tioga County Commissioner.

Dear Brian;

Remember on Feb. 23 when I talked to you and Roxie at the courthouse? I tried to get a letter from you stating that you were notified that I intended to apply for a permit to open those ditches on my property behind Jan Terry's house, and you told me the planning commissioner was the only one who knew anything about that and I would have to get a letter from him. Well Mr. No Name at D.E.R., Bureau of Dams & Waterway Management, P.O. Box 2357, Harrisburg, informed me that I must notify you, not him. Could you be so kind as to give me a letter stating you were notified on Feb. 23 so as not to delay the processing of my permit unnecessarily.

Thank you,

Francis Burnier

I drove into town and soon stood before Roxie. She had signed for the notification letter I had mailed certified, with a receipt requested, after my last visit. I didn't want to start an argument, so I said absolutely nothing as I handed her the letter. She didn't say anything either and soon disappeared into the rear office. After a few minutes she returned and went straight to the copy machine. When she handed my letter back to me it was stamped RECEIVED

MAR 7, 1988, and it was signed by Brian Edgecomb. I thought of asking her if she wanted to keep the original, but we had not even made eye contact since I handed her the letter. I didn't intend it as a whisper, but my diaphragm and vocal cords didn't coordinate properly to make it audible when I said, "Thank you," and I didn't give it a second try.

Chapter Ten

Wellsboro

Across the street from Matt Baker's office is a Green with the town's Winken Blinken and Nod Fountain. To the right of the Green is the courthouse. Looking left past the Baptist church you can see the hospital.

Surrounding Wellsboro is a mixture of farms, state-owned game lands, the Pennsylvania Grand Canyon, a golf course, and a small airport. The rustic setting of the town nestled in a basin in the hills provides a picture an active chamber of commerce uses to promote tourism. The diners and boutiques carry scenic postcards of local views both current and historical. (Among them is a card showing the fields of celery growing on fields now considered to be wetlands.)

The single high school which serves the community, the ecumenical element in its churches, and main street with it gas lights and stores all add to the small-town atmosphere. If your work takes you to the hospital or the courthouse, to a factory or store; if you are retired or are farming, or if you eat at the hotel or the diner, chances are pretty good you will contact the same people in more than one setting.

I don't want to give the impression that everyone was one happy family. There was the "flatlander vs. ridgerunner" rivalry. The way it appeared to me, if you were born and raised in Wellsboro, everyone else was a flatlander. If you were a hunter or tourist, everyone else was a ridgerunner. If you moved there as an adult you saw yourself as one of the "others."

The local Audubon Society has an active group of bird watchers. There is also a group of "environmental" watchers who call themselves the Pine Creek Headwaters Protection Group. Of course there was also the white collar/blue collar rivalry with all of it hues.

Mary and I attended the First Baptist Church, which had a mix of the above. Matt Baker and I played on the church softball team. Matt also worked as an aide for Representative Edgar Carlson and in the same office as Bill Hebe. On the ball field in sweat clothes or in the church pews wearing a tie and coat, I felt fairly comfortable talking to Matt, but in his office my collar was dark blue and Matt's was white. I couldn't escape the feeling that from his perspective I was a flatlander.

Matt Baker no longer conveyed the confidence he showed on my first visit when he told me he would make a few phone calls and straighten out the overzealous Corps. Instead he said in an apologetic tone, "There are some gray areas as to when a ditch can be cleaned. At the meeting in Harrisburg back in January—the one you were excluded from—I learned about some laws that quite honestly surprised me. Apparently wetlands are part of a very fragile ecological system and there are laws on the book...."

"I know, I know," I interrupted, "I have heard all that from the Corps, the E.P.A. and the D.E.R. But you know the history of this farm and that I'm not draining some virgin natural wetland, that is why I came to you to see if you can get some answers. I want to know if I do indeed need a permit to clean my ditches. I want to know where they get the idea that I drained one hundred acres. Why do they make these investigations on my property and then tell me it's not public information and they don't have to tell me what they were looking for or what they found? I want to know who determines what the water level should be in Marsh Creek. If they raise the road and put in a culvert to let the water out, can you clean the culvert? And of course, I sure wish I knew who turned me in."

Matt said, "These are all good questions. I can't answer them but if you put them in writing I will send them around to the people who can."

As I left his office, I paused on the steps and looked around. I remembered when we had bought the big house in the center of the wetlands. The closing had been in this same office. Bill Hebe was our attorney because he had represented us when we bought the farm. We signed the documents and gave them the check without questioning anybody. Then we sat in the car in front of the stairs and read the title document. We had known that Ron Lundgren was a previous owner, but when we read in the title that there was a right-of-way reserved to him, it didn't seem right. I went back in to get it straightened out. Hebe had left, but I didn't think he had done the paperwork anyway, so I was content to talk to the secretary. "I don't know why this right-of-way is reserved to Lundgren, but I don't want it on my deed. I own both properties and it may be moot but I thought the right-of-way was established so the cows could pass through this property from the pasture to the barn."

She said, "This deed has not yet been recorded, so it is good that you raise the question now." She disappeared into a back room for about ten minutes, and when she returned, she handed the title back to me. It had Ron Lundgren's name whited out. I knew he had continued to hunt ducks on the pond after he sold the house, but now that we were living there he would have to find another place to hold his shooting parties.

Just around the corner was Lynn Mader's law office. He was the lawyer I hired to have the deeds to our property changed from joint ownership to Mary's part and my part. I'm of the belief that if I was fined they would take just my property and let her keep hers. I remember him telling me he belonged to Ducks Unlimited. Belonging to Ducks Unlimited was the "in" thing to do for the influential set.

I later found it didn't make any difference whose name the titles bore.

Down the street a little way was the Penn Wells, where the lawyers ate their lunch at a certain table and, according to local belief, decided the court cases. I wondered if the wetland issue had been brought up at that infamous table and if it would do any good to put it in writing for Matt.

John Synder drove by in his Game Commission vehicle. He always seemed to not see me and my arm made it only halfway up when I waved to him.

Down the street was the library and art center. That was where the Pine Creek Headwater Protection Group held their first meeting on September 10, 1987. Mary and I had attended because we were involved tracking birds for the Audubon Society breeding bird atlas, and a lot of birders showed interest in the protection of the environment. At the close of the meeting they asked everyone to line up for the picture they were putting in the paper to show all the people who were going to help stop pollution. From what was said earlier about getting people to monitor the creek, I had the feeling they wanted to search out someone who was doing something they didn't like and report it to the D.E.R. In my mind there was enough common knowledge to go after the real polluters like the sewer plant and the factories in town. If I thought my neighbor's cow pooped too close to the creek, I would tell him so myself; I wouldn't turn him into the D.E.R. I told Mary if she wanted to get in the picture she could but I didn't think I would be joining the group.

Thinking about it later, I wondered again what the group's part in this might have been. Jack Cupper was chairman of the board of directors, and after the meeting he called me to see if I would go to a meeting to protest a proposed auto junkyard not too far from my house. He said I should tell them that rain could wash antifreeze into the creek if they had a junkyard that close to it. I told him I was busy myself that night and to see if he could find someone else to go for him.

The birders' meeting following my receipt of the registered letter was held at Cupper's house, and Synder was to talk on the care of injured birds. Since all of my efforts to contact Synder had been thwarted I seized the opportunity and went to the meeting. After John gave his presentation and people began to leave, I confronted him. I said, "If I have done something of which you don't approve, you can take this opportunity to tell me about it."

Snyder acted confused, so I said, "Do you know who I am?" When he didn't answer, I continued, "The name is Burnier and I don't have much respect for tipsters who are anonymous."

Snyder said, "I don't know what you are talking about."

"Well, if I ever do anything you don't like, just knock on my door and tell me." I emphasized it enough that some heads turned as people made their way to the door. Cupper didn't call to get a report for the bird atlas and Mary said she wasn't going to do any more birding with them. I didn't care one way or the other whether they knew which birds we observed living on our property.

I walked to where my car was parked behind the church. I had talked with different people at the church about my wetlands problem, but there were only a couple of farmers who attended and all I could get from the doctors, merchants, and the politically oriented members was a polite, "I'm sorry you can't use your land."

Don Knaus, who had connections with the Game Commission, said, "The people I talked to don't know why anyone is making such a big thing of it."

When I drove in my drive, Jim Thornton was there, and as we talked Howard Leber drove by. It reminded me of a time when Jim and I were talking wetlands soon after I got the Letter. Mary and I had been birding with the Lebers and we had discussed what I intended to do with the pond behind my house. They knew I wasn't out to destroy any duck pond. When my illegal drainage story hit the paper, Leber had stopped on his way by and asked, "Is there anything new with the Corps?" Before long he and Jim were arguing.

I had listened for a little while and said, "I hate to say this, but this looks like it is going to turn into a fight between the landowners and the environmentalists." At the time, I considered myself to be neutral, but this time as Leber drove by dressed in his park ranger uniform, I knew which side I was on.

The more I tried to convince people the Corps was wrong, the less effective I became. It seemed that no one had any sympathy for someone who felt he shouldn't have to sacrifice his property rights for the good of the people. The thing getting to me was that I wasn't convinced cleaning my ditch was harmful to anyone. I admitted that when the dam was in the creek and the sewage from town was backing up Webster's ditch and settling out over my land, it benefitted the people downstream. It just seemed to me if they couldn't fix the sewer plant, they should have at least been willing to rent my land. With the dam removed, the sewage was all going straight downstream anyway.

I was getting more and more discouraged. The choirs from the community churches participated in a concert. After the service, as I walked out the door in my choir robe, a dear lady from the Pine Creek Headwaters Protection Group spotted me and said, "I didn't know there was a good side to you."

Even my wife said, "Don't you think you are a little egotistical to think you're the only one who knows what is right?"

Then I talked to Rhonda Mcatee on the phone. She said, "I believe you. I understand what you are saying. I know the feeling. The same thing happened to us. We are having a meeting to gather support to fight this nonsense here in Waterford. I know it is an awful long way to drive but I would like to have you come."

I replied, "Just tell me how to find the place."

Jim and I found the school where the meeting was being held and parked the car. We found a door that opened for us, but looking around, we had no idea where the meeting was to be held. Three young ladies appeared and I asked, "Are one of you Rhonda?"

"No...why?"

"We are looking for a meeting of the North West Pennsylvania Land Owners." I said, "Rhonda said she would be here and I can't wait to give her a big hug."

"We are here for a volleyball game, but I think the meeting is in the auditorium down the next hall to the right. Have you met Rhonda yet?"

I confessed, "I have only talked to her on the phone, but I feel like the closest of kin."

The lady smiled just a little and said, "She is a very attractive woman."

I may have blushed just a little as I asked, "Do you know her?"

The reply came, "Yes. She is my cousin."

We found the meeting place and settled in about two-thirds of the way down the center aisle. After about ten minutes of watching stage hands set up microphones and furniture, people began arriving and taking scattered seats. When there were thirty or forty people settled, Rhonda walked in with her father and mother. All three had their arms loaded with papers and booklets. I needed no introduction—her cousin had understated her good looks. She scanned the auditorium and I rose and stood in the aisle. She was talking as she approached, "You must be Mr. Burnier." I nodded, and she continued as she offered her hand from under a load of papers, "I'm sorry we are late. So glad you could come."

"Bob Brace," her father said. We shook hands and he disappeared to the front of the hall.

Rhonda went on, "Do you want to tell me some details of your story or do you want to sit at the table with us to give your testimony?"

I had some written notes and I offered them to her. She glanced through them and said "Good, great, this is fine,...can you stick around after for a little while? We would like to talk with you, okay?"

Bob was rearranging some of the microphones. His wife Babe was at the door passing a handout to the stream of people coming in. This meeting was much more organized than I had expected. I went against the flow of people finding seats to where Babe stood and asked, "May I have one please?"

She handed me a set of papers which included an agenda of the night's meeting, some stories of people accused of wetland violations, and an advertisement to join the N.W.P.L.A. "I hope we get a chance to talk," she said, as she continued to pass out papers.

I returned to my seat. I hadn't felt this good since the registered letter arrived. Not only were these people understanding and sympathetic, they were doing what they could do to effect a change. I wasn't sure I agreed with everything everyone who had an ax to grind said, but I knew I was going to join. It felt great to know I was not alone after all.

Chapter Eleven

A Look in the File

No one at the *Wellsboro Gazette* would tell me where they got their information or who supplied the picture of Garskof and Bernhardy. Everyone in town denied any knowledge of why I had been selected as the destroyer of the environment. I had received no response from the letter I had given Matt. It still remained a puzzle to me that all those high-powered meetings and inspections that took place at my house were because of an anonymous tip. I remembered Martha Mitchell, and I knew a drunk with a phone could be a powerful thing, but this went beyond all reason.

I called Garskof and asked if his file was public information or if it was like the D.E.R. and all secret. Irwin replied, "I have nothing to hide. If you would like to look at your file we could arrange a time for you to do that."

I assured him, "It would be worth the peace of mind to take a day and drive down there just to see how this all came about."

I was really surprised to see how thick the stack of papers was Tom Pluto produced for my inspection. The first time I met Tom was when he conducted an information class on wetland identification at the Corps' Ives Run recreational area. When he told the group it would be too costly to identify and notify all the wetlands owners, I suggested they simply overlay an assessment map with a transparent wetland map and send a note with the tax bill to all those who could no longer use their land.

Tom knew I didn't feel I had the right to cause damage to my neighbor, but he also knew I was madder than a wet hornet about the notice of violation and being forced to plug my ditches.

"Here is some reading for you," Tom said, "if you are not through by lunch don't worry about it. I eat in the office anyway."

The top page on the stack was titled, "Telephone or Verbal Conversation Record."

Date: 10/23/87.
Person Calling: Dennis Bernhardy P.A. Game, Jersey Shore

Summary of Conversation: Game Commission was calling to report violation along Rt. 6 just outside of Wellsboro. ...Large marsh drainage by absentee owner who lives in Chicago. Dredged a main channel this summer with swamp dozer...also broke dike along Marsh Creek which drained 100+ acres in there according to Dennis. Owner worked all summer by hand, draining also.

I asked if he had phone #, address for property owner, Mr. Francis Burnier. He did not but would try to get.

He said that Greg Gabowitz will call/notify D.E.R. today.

Garskof

Garskof had been in an adjoining office, and when he walked by I said, "You could have looked in the phone book or called information for my phone number. Even if you were convinced I lived in Chicago there was only one Burnier to call and that would have been my son."

Garskof replied, "When the Game Commission failed to supply your number, I assumed it was unavailable."

Telephone record

Date: 11/4/87:

Mr. Terry wanted an update re. our action.

He indicated that this brother Scott could provide aerials or blowups of slides (at a cost) & could have him call me on Friday.

Garskof

It seemed a little ironic to me that if Terry was out to get me he would expect to get paid for supplying information.

I glanced at a few more "conversation" records and then came across the deposition form on which Garskof on November 17, 1987 had written the "Field Trip to Tioga County on 26 Oct. '87."

The single-spaced, two-page document was a mixture of, "According to Mr. Terry," "Mr. Terry indicated," "Photographs show," and "It appears." Some of it was true and some was false. There was a statement in the middle of the form which clearly stated, "We inspected the subject site, and could confirm that ditching had occurred on site." Those mentioned as being in attendance were Norma Klein (E.P.A.), Larry Copenhaver (D.E.R.), and Dennis Bernhardy (P.G.C.). There was no mention of U.S. Fish and Wildlife, Synder, or Hayden, and there was no mention of the press.

Telephone record:

Date: 12/9/87.

Dennis Bernhardy, P.G.C. calling.

Arnold Hayden—Lives in Wellsboro, is a biologist
with Game Commission. Knows Burnier wetlands very well.
Arnold has been living there for 25 years.

Telephone record:

Garskof calling Arnold Hayden.

Yes, Mr. Hayden is familiar with the Burnier property.
Nothing has been farmed there since he lived in area—27 years.

S.C.S. did drainage in muck area along Rt. 287 to help keep the Thornton celery fields dry (enough to farm) early 1970s. He doesn't remember any drainage over by Burnier at that time.

When they drained the "Wellsboro muck," Mr. Hayden feels that it was the worst environmental disaster in PA.—Area was a highly diverse wetland system/high wildlife diversity/values.

The date of these phone calls put them after the meeting at my house on November 24. The report was written up January 8, 1988, pretty much the way the Game Commission had described the history of my property. I wondered how much influence Hayden had on it. I knew Thronton would like to see what Hayden said about his land, and I asked, "Mr. Pluto, would it be possible to get a copy of some of these documents?"

Tom said, "Yes, sure. There is a jar of paper clips on the desk. Just put a paper clip on the ones in which you are interested."

I had a box full of letters and news items at home and there was no need to get copies of what I already had. I began at the beginning of the file and started putting paper clips on memos and reports that surprised me or substantiated my assumptions. I felt Garskof had summarized our phone conversations fairly accurately, and Terry's calls were so petty and redundant I put clips on only a couple of those memos.

Telephone record:

Date: 2/8/88. Garskof calling Norm Johnson.

I called to get some background info on the history of the site.

Some drainage work done by Webster in 1969 but Agnes hurricane in 1972 knocked out any plowing use of fields. (Webster had cows until 1978.) 1978-1980 rented to Howard Hazleton, 1981-1986 rented to Jim Thornton.

Fields in question probably only had some hay cut off of them (i.e., not in corn) maybe as late as 1980 but he wasn't sure.

1969 farm plan show fields as "cropland" with some unspecified acreage as perennial hay i.e., reed canary grass. Yes, reed canary grass could have been permanent vegetation on these particular fields.

Norm had showed me a copy of the history of the farm that he had prepared from the S.C.S. records to present on my behalf at the Harrisburg meeting January 28, so I was puzzled not only by the date but the watered-down version (pun intended).

I put a clip on one dated April 8, 1988.

Telephone record:

Roger Lehman, PA. Game Com. calling.

Willis and Roger Lehman were up yesterday and saw area. John Snyder saw him out with a piece of equipment.

What seemed funny about this was when I had heard that Roger had purchased the wetlands for Ducks Unlimited, I had called him to see if he was interested in my land, but he said he didn't know me or my land.

I used a couple more paper clips and the jar was getting near empty. My interest was mostly on the early parts of the file and most of what I was reading now wasn't very surprising. I began to scan the remaining papers and told Tom, "I have clips on the ones I would like copied. If there are too many I can narrow it down some."

Tom picked up the folder and fanned the papers to expose the clips. "That is okay. I can make copies of these." Tom said, "Did you find what you were looking for?"

"Well, actually I guess I have to go the Game Commission to find out how this got started," I said as I reached for my jacket, "But what I didn't find was the report on the Harrisburg meeting."

"That was a general meeting and we didn't discuss your case so it's not in your file, but I have a copy right here if you want to see it."

I read, "The purpose of the meeting was to explain the regulatory program with regards to wetlands, and in particular, how these regulations impact upon conversion or 'wet' areas to productive agricultural use.

"After introductions, I outlined the federal program with particular attention to farming exemptions. I explained how and why wetlands which may have been 'historically' farmed could be regulated by our program, and how and why these wetlands were excluded from the farming exemptions. I emphasized (along with D.E.R. and U.S.F.W.S.) that the purpose and intent of Section 404 was not to regulate areas which were actively farmed, which was a major concern of the farmer's representatives."

This was written up February 4, four days before the call to Norm.

I don't know if Garskof could see I was getting ready to leave or if he had other business to discuss with Tom, but he appeared and seemed interested in my reaction to what I had found. I said, "You seem to find it easier to believe Terry's and the Game Commission's lies than the truths I tell you."

Irwin started choosing his words. "When anyone calls me with information I assume they are telling me the truth. I have no reason to question their integrity...it is my job to protect the ecology as best I can."

I got the feeling right away that he wasn't going to apologize or bad-mouth the Game Commission. He went on, "Sometimes I am forced to evaluate conflicting testimony where I don't know who is telling the truth. In these situations I have a tendency to favor what is best for the ecology. There are a lot of people out there who don't care if they destroy the environment. I am not saying you are one of them, but it has to be stopped."

I started talking before he finished. "That is the problem I have with this. What I am doing isn't nearly as bad as what others do, yet I'm the one who is supposed to save the environment. Why don't you go after Jack Cupper, the head of the Audubon Society, for having a bulldozer sculpture a pond in his wetlands, or the preacher at the First Baptist Church for filling in the wetlands in his yard?"

Irwin replied, "I can't go after people I don't know about."

"I was told that Cupper's violation was reported," I retorted.

"If it was I should have a record of it," came the reply.

"Let's look at your records," I said.

We went into his office, and in a matter of seconds, Irwin said, "Here it is. It had indeed been reported, but the investigation was tabled on the recommendation of Game Commission personnel who inspected the site."

"Did you look at it?"

"No."

"Cupper is in Texas now, but why don't you call him and ask him what he did? He doesn't feel he did wrong any more than I do, and he will probably tell you what he did if you ask him."

"I don't have a Texas phone number recorded."

"I will get it for you," I promised.

Garskof restored the file and I turned toward the door. "This has proven to be very informative. I want to thank you for your cooperation."

Tom responded, "Glad to help."

"I would like to talk to the Game Commission at Jersey Shore, so I had better go now."

Then Tom asked, "Still think you should be compensated for your land?"

I replied, "I don't think I should have to bear the burden alone." I then added, "But I don't feel alone anymore. I talked to the Braces from around Erie and they also believe if the government wants their land, it should buy it."

"You don't want to get involved with those people," Tom said. "They are a bunch of contractors and oil people who want to make a big profit on wetlands."

"I don't know about that or what their land is worth, but I know my land could have been purchased for one dollar more than I paid for it and after all the labor I put into it I don't believe I should have to donate it to the ducks or their hunters."

Tom said, "Maybe we will have to take one-half of the defense budget and buy up the wetlands."

Jersey Shore

Walking down the hall, I looked into Dennis Bernhardy's office and he recognized me right off. "Mr. Burnier," he said.

"Mr. Bernhardy," I replied, "did the Corps call and warn you I was coming?"

"No. Should they have?"

"I just came from there and the earliest record they have is of the Game Commission calling them. I would like to find out where the complaint originated."

"We don't keep the same kind of files as the Corps, but I will help you as much as I can."

I asked, "Do you keep any kind of a log or diary."

He took out a book and asked, "Where should I start?"

"Start about October 26, 1987, and work back from there," I suggested.

"That was the trip out to inspect your property."

"Fine, and before that?"

"The twenty-fifth was Sunday, the twenty-fourth Saturday—the twenty-third was the day I talked to Garskof on the phone about the complaint we received about a possible wetland violation."

"Okay. Good. Now what do you have for the twenty-second and twenty-first?"

"That is strange—there are some pages missing. I don't know where they could have gone. And frankly, I can't remember. I will say this; we were acting on a complaint."

I took a deep breath, exhaled through closed lips, and said, "I realize it is getting near quitting time, but if you ever find the missing pages, let me know."

I never heard from Dennis, but Norm called and said, "You are listed on the agenda for the January [26, 1989] meeting of the Tioga County Conservation District along with Irwin Garskof. He is to give instruction on how and when to enforce the new wetland laws."

"That is funny," I replied, "Garskof said that Pat from the Corps' permit division was going to set up an appointment with me for the twenty-sixth. I have not heard form her yet, so if she calls, I will tell her I will have to work it in around this meeting."

I hung up and called Garskof, but I got an answering machine. I left a message with Jack Cupper's Texas phone number. I also left word that Pat had not yet contacted me about a meeting.

January 24

Pat called to tell me she could not make the meeting on the twenty-sixth. I asked if Garskof was still coming and she said, "No."

At the meeting on the twenty-sixth Commissioner Edgcomb said, "Garskof called this morning and said he has the flu and can't attend the meeting."

Listed under "old business" on the agenda for the February meeting was simply "wetlands." Garskof arrived about halfway through the treasure's report and asked if there was a slide projector closer than the one in his car. Mr. Edgcomb dispatched someone to the commissioners' offices and I caught Irwin's eye and nodded in acknowledgement. When the messenger returned and presented Garskof with the projector, Irwin left the room. Soon he returned and after a brief whispered talk with Brian, Brian said, "There will be a short recess for an executive meeting."

The commissioners disappeared into the hallway with Garskof. When they returned to the room about ten minutes later, Brian said, "For those of you who have come for the wetlands presentation, I want to inform you that it will not be today. Mr. Garskof was not aware that this was a public meeting and he is not authorized to give public presentations."

They resumed where they had been on the agenda, and when Garskof packed up and left, I followed him out the door and said, "You must have an hour of so that isn't scheduled. I could show you where Cupper lives."

Irwin took a deep breath and let his chin drop on his chest as he exhaled, paused, cocked his head toward me, and with his eyes closed, said, "Why not?"

I touched the ferns and bushes that looked like the ones in my famous field as we walked around Cupper's pond. Apparently I didn't overplay my hand because Irwin said, "Yes it's wetlands...what do you want me to do?"

"I think you should write him a letter and tell him that filling in a wetland is a no-no, and if he fills any more, you will get the attorney general after him."

Irwin said, "I will. I will send him a letter if you want me to."

"Well, I figure what is good for the goose is good for the gander," I replied.

Finally, on April 12, 1989, a wetlands forum was held in Wellsboro. Brian Edgcomb, chairman of the Tioga County Commissioners and Conservation District, began the meeting by saying, "First of all, I would like to ask that everyone conduct themselves in a orderly manner. Specifics and axes to grind cannot be tolerated."

I took that personally and translated it to mean, "If you raise your voice I will kick you out."

"First of all, representing the Baltimore District of the Army Corps of Engineers, we have Thomas Philip, the third—excuse me the second—assistant chief of the Corps' regulatory branch."

After a few ice-breaking remarks, Mr. Philip said, "First of all, I would like to give you an overview of the whole program to give everyone an idea of what it is about and where we are today. Way back in the late 1800s, Congress passed a law which got Congress involved in the waters."

I listened again to how the Corps was dragged, kicking and screaming, into their present regulatory position. How they were the only ones who knew how to build bridges to protect the shipping industry on the Mississippi. How the law was expanded to include not only the course and flow, but the condition of the water, so now you needed a permit to dump sewage into navigable waters. Philip went on to explain how the Corps was forced to expand the navigable waters to include headwaters, and finally in 1984, to include all wetlands. How a problem remained because everybody had a different definition of a wetland. I paid particular attention as Tom said, "Well, I am happy to say that in December of '88— and finally signed in January 5 of '89—the five major agencies of federal government that deal with wetlands agreed on a single common wetland delineation manual that the federal government will use, and if it falls within the purview of that manual, it is a wetland and it is regulated."

Mr. Philip went on to explain how Congress looked on farmers as being special and that as long as they didn't change the use or put fill in the wetlands, they didn't need a permit. It sounded to me that he hedged a little by saying if you were planting corn and changed to soybeans, that was a change of use and plowing was considered filling.

I sat through the presentation of the U.S. Fish and Wildlife Service and the Wetlands and Marine Policy Section of the E.P.A. without taking any notes.

Willis Sneath, the regional director of the North Central Division of the Pennsylvania Game Commission, had some interesting things to say. "We...our field people kinda act as the eyes and the ears for the other departments who do not have somebody out in the local area...." I didn't have any trouble translating that: Synder and Hayden supply the fuel for the fire.

After talking about the Game Commission's interest in purchasing a local piece of property encumbered with a covenant that provided for the drainage of the adjacent land (Thornton) for the purpose of farming, he said, "I am not a legal expert enough to determine whether that old deed restriction back in 1901...the new laws relating to wetlands override that or not...that maybe would be something that would have to be resolved in the courts as a final disposition." That was easy to translate too: If the Game Commission got hold of the parcel of land, Thornton was through growing vegetables unless he had a lot of money for lawyers.

Roger Fickes, the wetlands coordinator for the D.E.R., talked about the Dams and Encroachments Act, and John Arway of the Pennsylvania Fish Commission told us about his concern for each and every fish, salamander, snake, and tadpole that live in the State of Pennsylvania.

When John said, "In closing, I would like to turn the meeting back over to Brian," I raised my hand as high as I could and held it there while Brian boasted about how Tioga County was "environmentalist before it was fashionable" and gave the ground rules for the questions and answer part of the program.

"Francis, you are on first. You have had your hand up for quite a while, buddy."

I rose to my feet, "Well I was pleased to see that in the beginning you announced this wouldn't be specifics, but I see that Tom Philip talked about Baltimore, so I would like to talk about Wellsboro. Tom went back to the 1800s with the water laws on the Mississippi, so I'll go back too. Mr. Sneath talked about a 1901 agreement, but on my property I would like to go back to the late 1800s. Before this farm was sold, the previous owner recorded a mutual agreement in the courthouse which gave him drainage rights and his brother passage rights. These guys realized that, number one; if you could not maintain access to your land it wasn't worth much, and number two; if you could not maintain drainage, your land wasn't worth much.

"Tom tells us that the steamboat law that started one hundred years ago in Baltimore has changed over the years, so now this year it includes every wet spot in Wellsboro and the drainage rights we have in our deeds are worthless. I think it is just about time that some of these questions are addressed. We have a stream called Marsh Creek that, if I may be specific, goes through my property. The 1901 covenant Sneath talked about addresses parts of Marsh Creek and mandates that it be kept cleaned. When cars are dumped in there, they slow the flow and causes silt to elevate the creek bed. My question is this: What is the proper elevation of the creek bed? I know you have had an opportunity to think about the answer because I wrote the Corps a letter months ago and asked about it."

Mr. Philip said he got so much mail he wasn't able to read it all and he never saw my letter, and this was not the place to talk about my specific case.

Steve Priset said, "I am a neighbor of Mr. Burnier and what he does with his land affects my land. I would like to know why you don't ask his neighbors what they would like to see him do with his property. The Game Commission tells you what some guy who drives up here from Philly wants and that is important to you, but you are not interested in what we his neighbors want."

Mr. Philip answered, "Again, I don't want to talk about a specific case I know nothing about."

Someone asked, "Is it the Corps' policy not to inform the property owner about the inspections and that there is a formal report being filed on him by the Corps?"

Tom Philip said, "No! If you weren't told, that is wrong. Our records are public records—except our enforcement records, which are sealed until a judge bangs the gavel in the case, for the protection of the person who may be accused of the violation. That would be assuming guilt before it was ever tried by a judge."

Brian said, "I appreciate hearing that, because that has been a problem here in Tioga County."

Mr. Besancency asked, "Could you expand on what the roadmasters can do regarding cleaning ditches?"

Both Roger Fickes and Dave Putman gave assurances that township supervisors and roadmasters would not have any problems with cleaning ditches.

Arnold Borden, the Delmar Township supervisor said, "What are you supposed to do with the dirt when you take it out of one of those ditches?"

Dave Putman said, "Don't put it in a wetland."

"What the hell are you going to do with it? How are you going to get rid of it?"

"You are talking about sidecasting the material?"

"Right. What are you going to do with it?"

"You can't sidecast it into the swamp without a permit."

"But my book says I have a right to clean that ditch."

"That is true. In a case like that you can get a permit—"

"I have been trying for a year to get a permit."

That went in circles for a while and the question never did get answered.

"I am Steve Thornton. I represent Northeastern Farm Credit. We have about twenty million dollars worth of loans out in this county, primarily to farmers. About $130 million across the northern tier here...I am hearing a couple of things here...that there isn't a problem with agriculture. I hear Mr. Snead from the Game Commission saying that there may be instances where the federal laws supersede the local deeds and covenant. My question is—and I don't know who to ask—as a lender it scares me when someone starts to question how legal someone's deed is. That is understandable—we have mortgages on deeds. It is our organization's position that if you are going to take something away from a farmer, you have got to compensate him for the loss of use of that land. We place a mortgage on a property, and the fellow is going to repay it, obviously, from the fruits of the land. You basically tell him he can't use that land. He's got to have some way to make his payment or he defaults on his mortgage, leaving me as the mortgage lender with what—although it may have great wildlife value—it ain't worth diddly squat to sell to anyone else."

Steve told me before the meeting that he couldn't talk from a farmer or neighbor point of view because he was at work and representing Farm Credit. He even sat across the room from his father and me. When he talked about Snead and the deeds, I told his dad, "He veiled that pretty good."

Even if Tom Philip didn't have prior knowledge of names and specific local concerns, Putman apparently did. Putman said, "Let me answer that...there is always a way to get something done. If you want to drain farm "A" and it goes across swamp "B" to place "D," and the normal maintenance is to cut a ditch, one alternative is to run a solid pipe through there so that it wouldn't drain the area in the middle."

A person unknown to me said, "In flooding of a wetland—if it changes the ecosystem—we know the Corps does it, we see it on

TV all the time. We are talking of one-half or one-quarter acre, and we see thousands of acres the Corps is flooding."

Philip said, "Every major Corps dam project is demanded...by Congress."

"Are we going to find it harder to get a pond permit?"

"My office doesn't like to see wetlands flooded by a pond."

This kind of double-talk went on and on. The fourth or fifth question after Brian had said there would be one more was asked by Thornton.

"On your permit there I see a place for trickery. Can you explain that?"

"For what?"

"Trickery."

"Trickery?"

"Trickery. On your permit it says 'trickery.'"

I thought I would help them out. "Near the end of the joint permit application form, Item eighteen I believe. Can I ask one more question?"

Brian said, "Yes, go ahead, Francis, while we are looking up trickery."

"I get the impression that wetlands are good to have—am I wrong in this?"

"No, you are right."

"Okay. They tell me that if that culvert under Webster Road causes my pasture to become wetlands, that it doesn't matter why it became wetlands. If it is wetlands I can't use it anymore."

Dave Putman said, "Let me say this: It is not going to turn into wetlands overnight."

"No, no. I'm not saying overnight, but once it has the cattails, then it's wetlands. Do you agree?"

"Yes."

"Okay. Let me ask you this: The D.E.R. is supposed to take over the management of the railroad. They are one of the biggest proponents of wetlands in the state. If they fail to maintain the culverts, the railbed will act as a dam and turn everything above it into wetlands." Then I went further than I should have by adding, "Are you going to tell the people of Asaph that you are going to take over their land?"

Putman said, "Now you are grasping at straws. It just doesn't happen."

I said, "Grasping at straws? Don't tell me it doesn't happen."

I guess I had begun to raise my voice, because Brian took charge and said, "It is after four o'clock and I have to cut this off here. They indicated they would talk specifics with you after the meet-

70

ing. I would like to thank those who participated in today's program. If any of you still have questions, put them in writing to me and I will see that they are addressed to the proper people."

As the public left, I got out a permit application form and read again; "18 U.S.C. Section 1001 provides that: Whoever, in any manner within the jurisdiction of any department or agency of the United Stated knowingly falsifies, conceals, or covers up by any trick, scheme, or device a material fact or makes any false, fictitious or fraudulent statement or entry, shall be fined not more than $10,000 or imprisoned not more than five years, or both."

I approached Roger Fickes and asked what they had decided about Thornton's "trickery" question. He told me it applied to the people applying for the permit, but not to the people opposed to it.

I talked with Tom Philip for quite a while.

I said, "Fill is something that raises the level. I didn't put any fill anywhere."

Tom replied, "Even if what you shoveled out of your ditch disseminated, it would add a tiny fraction of a centimeter to the level—it wouldn't just disappear."

"If you are worried about that little amount, you had better clean out the creek. Every time it rains hard, the creek overflows and many times that much fill settles out on my fields."

"I don't think you understand—I can help you."

"I am not looking for help. All I want to know is what I can do with my land."

We didn't get very far. He kept trying to get me to admit to some wrong and I kept trying to get him to prove it or at least explain what the wrong was. I wasn't going to buy this fill stuff he kept talking about. Some guy I assumed to be his chauffeur said, "You don't have to talk so loud."

I looked around. There were only four or five people there besides the janitor, who keep hitting his broom into the pews with an echoing thud.

"I am sorry if it offends you," I said in about the same tone. "I come from a large family and that is just the way I talk when I am trying to make a point."

He turned to Tom and said, "I have plans for tonight. Let's go."

Near the end of May I received a letter of denial on my permit application. It appeared to me to be a mixture of personalized and generic paragraphs rehashing the same old points of contention. I answered the letter.

Dear Mr. Sauer:
I read your letter of denial and have become even more

71

confused. I contacted a lawyer and he asked me what I thought I could do with my property. I told him I didn't know. In the first place, my application was to clean my ditches and was made only because of threats of fines, not because I thought my situation required a permit. The discharge of fill material into wetlands is something your people concocted.

In the second place, I am not proposing to convert a farm area into a use to which it was not previously subject. There are maps, farm records, pictures, and testimony in your file that prove this land has historically been farmed and cropped.

In the third paragraph, you reference letters received from the E.P.A., U.S.F.W.S., and the Pennsylvania Game Commission. There again confusion is created because of people making statements based on erroneous information and assumptions. Nevertheless, at Mr. Rugiel's request I replied to those letters.

In reply to your fourth paragraph, let me refer you to the Federal Register Vol. 51, 323.4 and ask you to note the part on minor drainage and plowing. If you were told you could comb your hair in the bathroom and eat in the kitchen, but you could not use any plumbing or any appliances, you would have to concur that would be a viable use. The difficulty in storing perishables and preparing food, not to mention the bathing and other hygienic functions that must be altered, would make the idling of the common conveniences seem a bit absurd.

If (33 cfr 320.4 (b) (4)) simply states that no permit will be granted which involves the alteration of important wetlands, could you explain what is going on at Cowanesque Lake?

Please send me a copy of the 40cfr so I can familiarize myself with (404) (B) (1) Guidelines.

In July of 1988, Matt Baker, district aide for Edgar Carlson, wrote Mr. Rugiel and asked if he would provide specific answers and information for my questions, which included: Do I need a permit to clean my ditches? (323.4) Does the

Corps still allege that I placed fill material in wetlands? (323.2 (e)) What is the level at points between Wellsboro and Pine Creek that Marsh Creek was supposed to be cleaned? You responded in September 1988 with a letter that wasn't very clear to me. I asked Mr. Baker if he could interpret your answers more precisely, but he too thought your answers were a bit evasive. What Mr. Baker did say was that the Corps was deferring the enforcement lead to the D.E.R.

Even though I am not on Mr. Carlson's staff I had questions, and I called John P. O'Hagan as you suggested. His office told me to call Mr. Rugiel. Frank Plewa answered the phone and told me to call Mr. Garskof. I was then told to call Mr. Pluto, and Frank Plewa answered the phone and told me Mr. Pluto was not available.

When D.E.R. sent me the permit I opened the plug in the ditch. Then I got a registered letter from Mr. Rugiel telling me I couldn't do anything without D.A. approval.

If I can use the land for pasture, can I clean the ditches to keep it from being (remaining) flooded?

Since I tried to call you and found you were no longer involved, I'm sure you will pass this to the proper person. Tom Philip said something about a Tucker Act. Please send me information on how to appeal.

Thank you

Francis Burnier

Chapter Twelve

Addendum

Conrail had been granted an abandonment of the line that transverses our valley and the rails had been removed. The D.E.R. was negotiating for use of the right-of-way for a recreational trail. My neighbors, who lived on the high side of the railbed, were concerned.

Priset maintained a dairy operation, and he told me the ditches in his pasture needed cleaning. I told him he should get Conrail or the D.E.R. to clean the ditch along the railbed and I would clean the sediment in the pasture ditches. He thought that if he pulled the tree branches, rail ties, and telephone poles out of the railbed ditch, it would provide enough drop for freshly cleaned pasture ditches.

It wasn't long after those ditches were cleaned that another neighbor knocked on my door. Randy told me he had tried to get a loan on his property but could not because it had become too wet. Randy had sold his cows and moved away because of his job. He was planning to return after a few years to live, but he was here for just a week to get the house ready for the new renters. I looked at the drainage system and could see it was currently being drained to a point upstream from its originally designed discharge point. He told me that the rail ditch had become clogged for such a distance that he went the short route uphill. I pictured in my mind that any high water within three feet of the creek bank would flood his field. I tried to discourage him.

"Those cattails qualify this as a wetland." I tried to sound authoritative.

"They are just in the low-lying parts of the field, and that is what I want to eliminate," Randy replied. "That is why I can't get a loan."

"But you just can't go around draining wetlands anymore," I offered.

"I saw what you did at Priset's and you aren't in jail. What is the difference? I had cows on this field before and as soon as I move back I will have cows again."

"I agree with you; just because you let the land lie a few years it shouldn't make a difference, but—"

"Then you will do it?"

"I wouldn't feel comfortable draining it backwards."

"Then go the long way, and I will get someone to clean the junk out of the rail ditch like Priset did. What do you think it will cost?"

"About one thousand dollars if I decide to do it."

"I'm prepared and willing to pay you twice that."

"I didn't say I would, but if I do, I won't charge you double."

"I will be back up in six weeks. If you decide to do it, just go ahead because I want it done."

Ron Bellinger's back had been bothering him, and he asked what I thought of cleaning his pasture ditches. I owed Ron some favors and I knew he had had cows in that field since I moved to Pennsylvania.

"As long as you intend to keep it in pasture I don't see any problem," I intoned.

"I have had cows in there for the last fourteen years, and I don't own a cornplanter," Ron replied.

When the railroad was built in the 1800s, the course of Marsh Creek was changed. The upper part of the pasture drained into the old creek bed, which went through the corner of Ron's property. This was where the ditch along the railbed crossed under the bridge and joined the existing Marsh Creek. I could see where Priset had cleaned the trash out all the way down to there.

Originally another ditch had begun at a swale that ran diagonally from the road to the railbed in the lower part of Ron's pasture. That ditch had recently been filled by the railroad, and Ron had been draining the swale to the old creek bed ever since. I walked up a ditch in the swale, and when I reached the road I tied a red rag on the fence directly above the culvert that emptied into it.

School House Run passed through some state-owned lands above Ron's. I told him, "When I clean this property-line ditch, I will cast the spoil along the fence to make a dike. If they complain about making the state's land wetlands, tell them we will clean out the run to the creek like it is supposed to be. That would be better than having them complain that we drained their land against their wishes."

I cleaned the ditches and left the digger along the fence by the state land. I went to Chicago for a few days, and when I returned there was a tri-color contact paper note affixed to my door. It had a red border and large red capital letters that said. NOTICE. Then printed in black, smaller sized capital lettering: ANY WORK INVOLVING THE DISCHARGE OF DREDGED OR FILL MATERIAL ON THIS PROPERTY MAY REQUIRE A DEPARTMENT OF THE ARMY AND/OR STATE DEPARTMENT OF ENVIRONMENTAL RESOURCES PERMIT. A double space and, UNLESS YOU HAVE A VALID PERMIT. Another double space and, IMMEDIATELY CALL THE U.S. FISH AND WILDLIFE SERVICE (814) 234-4090. The bottom line of the printed sign read, NOTICE #   DATE   INVESTIGATOR. Handwritten with a felt pen was, Tioga #1, 5/24/91," and "Bill Savage," and outside the red border, "Please contact us regarding the work you performed at the Bellinger property. Urgent."

I called, "Is Bill Savage there, please?"

"No, Bill is away for a few days. Can I take a message?"

"I am reading a notice that was left at my house and it says 'call immediately' and 'urgent.' Apparently it has something to do with some ditches I am cleaning for a neighbor. I don't believe a permit is needed to clean ditches in a pasture, so I would like to discuss this with someone."

"All I can say is, don't do any more there until this is settled."

"Well, get out your rule book and let's get it settled," I said.

"No, I won't discuss it further on the phone. You will have to wait until Mr. Savage returns."

"Sorry, I guess I misinterpreted the 'call immediately' and 'urgent' in your notice."

I hung up and called Ron. He said, "They are going to come out and look at what you did. They said something about putting the ditches in too long and too deep, and they want them filled back in."

"Let me know when they are coming. In the first place, they have to get the Corps or the D.E.R. to make you do something—all the Fish and Wildlife Service can do is recommend. Unless you lied to me about keeping your cows, I don't think we did any thing illegal."

It was June 12 when Garskof arrived with U.S. Fish personnel in a vehicle escorted by the Pennsylvania State Police. The first thing they did was serve Ron with a search warrant. Then they proceeded to open maps and aerial photographs while the police officer stood behind all of us. The Fish people pointed out the differences in the photographs to Garskof and talked about how the most recent one (which was taken with my digger there) showed the ditches extending all the way to the road. Garskof seemed to agree with their analysis and I assumed he hoped to solidify it by looking at the other photos. It was evident, however, that the Fish people had selected the one of the five in which the ditches appeared the shortest.

Garskof had his soil probe and a ruler and said, "Let us take a closer look," and he headed off toward the place where the swale ditch was tapped to run into the old creek bed. I kept up with Garskof, Ron and his wife were paired with the Fish people, and Officer Friendly took up the rear. I reminded Garskof of the pictures of my neighbor's yard, which he had identified as wetlands almost four years before at my house. Garskof handed the ruler to the male member of the Fish people and said, "Let's get some measurements of the depth of the ditches."

I watched as the ruler was placed next to a high spot on the ditch berm and the numbers read off as Irwin took notes. I said, "If you want to get a reading of the true depth of the ditches, I have some maple syrup tubing you could use for a level. Ron has been cleaning these ditches by hand for the last fourteen years and building up this berm with the spoil."

Irwin said, "There is evidence of some ponding at this end."

In response, I addressed Ron, "Ron, show Mr. Garskof where the railroad filled in that ditch!"

The two of them disappeared to the railbed, and I studied the ditch berms. It was no mystery to me that the more sediment cleaned, the higher the berm. As I looked toward the place where I had tied the red rag, I could see that the berm got lower and lower. I concluded that either Ron had been a little lazy or because it was a wet water culvert, it hadn't needed cleaning to keep the pasture drained. When they returned, Garskof said, "We have the depth of the ditches recorded, now let's see if their length has been extended."

We walked about halfway to the road, and they took out the map they claimed proved their contention that the ditch had ended there. I winked at Ron and said, "Let's investigate further to see if we can find some evidence of a ditch. I might have dug a little deep, but you can see by the spoil the old ditch went farther than this." I kicked a clod and the native soil and ditch residue separated, revealing an old shoelace.

Finding foreign objects to point out became more difficult, and the group started to angle away from the ditch toward the cars. I hurried to the fence and said, "Look at this." While holding the weeds to the side to expose the culvert, I asked rhetorically, "Where do you supposed the tail ditch is?" I started gloating just a tad. "You didn't have to send a reconnaissance plane over to take pictures, I would have told you what I did if you would have talked to me when I called in response to your notice. Now tell me: Can you clean existing ditches in a pasture or can't you?"

Garskof said, "I will write up my findings and you will be notified as to what action will be required of you. I don't foresee anything major."

Barb Bellinger told me after they left, "I bet if you hadn't run the D.E.R. off of your property they wouldn't have said anything about this."

She was referring to the argument I had with the D.E.R. before going to Chicago. They had built a barricade across the right-of-way on my property while I was at work. I took the keys out of their tractor and told them they could have them back when they agreed to remove the barricade. I was sued and the judge made me give them back the keys.

We never did hear from the Corps, but two and a half months later I received a notice of violation from the D.E.R. telling me I was to notify them within thirty days of my intentions to backfill the ditches on Bellinger's property.

I told Ron, "It is your property and I am not going to fill them in unless you tell me to."

Ron said, "You are the one they are after. That is what they told Barb when they made the inspection."

I said, "If you ain't worried, I ain't worried."

Epilogue

Author's View

I was a linebacker for the Steinmetz High School football team. We had gone undefeated and if we won our remaining game with Harrison, we would qualify for the public league playoffs. Our regular quarterback had suffered a dislocated shoulder and did not dress for the game, making a strong defensive game of more importance.

One of the men on the three-man officiating team did not arrive on time, and the game was started with one official in the offensive backfield and one in the defensive backfield. Harrison drove down the field using predominantly a belly option series against which we had never before played. With a third down and two yards to go for a touchdown, we concentrated on stopping the play for a loss. I shot the hole at the snap of the ball and tackled the ball carrier just the way I was coached: reverse the forward progress with the shoulder pads, wrap with the arms and lock the hands, and continue to drive back until the whistle blows or the ball carrier is dumped on his backside. We hit the left hash mark on the ten yard stripe as the whistle sounded.

Our defensive adjustments were being fined-tuned and their biggest and best lineman played on the left side. I felt confident anticipating fourth and four from the left hash mark.

The marking of forward progress had thus far been erratic, and I was curious to see exactly where the ball would be placed. When the referee started toward the goal post I told him, "Hey, leave the ball on the hash mark!" He retraced a couple of steps and then turned away and said, "It is not your option as to where to place the ball for an extra point attempt."

I responded with, "That was no touchdown," which resulted in a yellow flag assessed on the kickoff.

We lost, and when we turned in our equipment, my coach said he talked to the official at a party and got this explanation: He had been fooled by the ball handling, and without a head linesman to mark the spot of the ball, he looked to the other official for help. He happened to have his hands under his armpits because his fingers were cold. That was interpreted as no opposition to a touchdown ruling. Once the touchdown signal was given and the flag thrown, the cold-fingered official wasn't going to overrule the touchdown call even though he didn't agree with it.

I was on third base with the tying run for our church softball team when the batter hit the ball back over the middle. The pitcher reached up and deflected the ball into the air. I retagged the base and took off for home. The ball was caught without ever touching the ground and an appeal was made at third. I was called out for leaving too early. When I told the umpire I didn't have to wait for the ball to be caught, only until it was touched, I was ejected from the game.

These kind of experiences are offered as proof of my inability to get along with those in authority. I read of John Pozagai being fined $202,000 and serving a three-year prison sentence for being a stubborn man and a willful and knowing criminal to the environment. I saw Rodney King being beaten, and I read that the police had reason to continue as they did because he kept getting up. I have no argument with those who take the position that maintaining law and order is important, but I do wonder: If Galileo lived today, would he suffer the same fate?

Speech to Congress

Federal Wetlands Hearing
Feb. 28, 1990

Thank you for the opportunity to give testimony as you consider the wetland issue.

My wife Mary, three of our six children, and I moved to a farm in Pennsylvania in 1984. Mary had grown up on the farm and helped her father farm it and the surrounding land before going to school in Chicago, where we met and married.

In 1986 we bought an adjacent farm that had been farmed since the 1800s. An elaborate system of dikes, gates, and drains had been installed by the turn of the century to grow vegetables. The Websters then bought some cows in 1947. The neglect of Marsh Creek made the vegetable operation ever more risky, and the conversion to a dairy operation was completed. In 1969 the Websters updated their farm plan and at that time designated fifty acres, most of which had been prime cropland, for wildlife in exchange for government assistance in relocating the drainage ditches on remaining cropland. With the Agnes flood in 1972, Marsh Creek became clogged with trash and drainage became even more difficult. Due to health reasons, the Websters sold their cows in 1978 and leased their land to Hazelton. The farm was then sold on contract to Oesterland, who leased it to Thornton Dairy Farms.

Everyone said this was a good farm. The one drawback was that because of the rich muck soil, the ground became very unstable when saturated with water, and the ditches would have to be cleaned before the land could be worked. I knew about the cars, the tractor tires, and the washing machines, the trees, and the other flood trash in Marsh Creek which caused this land to flood with any heavy rain, yet I was willing to clean the ditches by hand so a flood would be temporary and the adverse effect on corn or hay would be acceptable. We purchased the land and I immediately began cleaning the ditches. I didn't punch a clock, but I estimate I spent over one thousand hours of back-aching work cleaning them.

Then in the fall of '87 I started getting letters. First the Department of the Army sent me a letter saying I was in violation of section 404 of the Clean Water Act by placing dredged fill material in wetlands, even though by their own definition I didn't put any fill anywhere.

Then I received a letter from the E.P.A. saying I was in violation of Section 301 of the Clean Water Act by discharging pollutants into the nation's waters, and that the E.P.A. might pursue criminal prosecutions which could entail imprisonment and fines of fifty thousand dollars per day. I live downstream from the village sewer plant and I had the water tested as it came out of my ditch and as it came onto my property from upstream. The test showed that the water coming down the creek had two hundred times as much of what the laboratory called fecal coliform as that coming out of my ditch.

Then I received a notice of violation from the D.E.R. saying I was in violation of section 693.6 of the Dam Safety and Encroachments Act when I opened my existing ditches. After being charged with filling and polluting, I was told my crime was cleaning a ditch. Because 693.6 makes it a violation to maintain or abandon, I was at a loss to know if I should clean or not clean all the old ditches on my farm. I even asked Roger Fickes—if cleaning was maintaining, what was abandoning? He didn't know.

I learned that the hay field was considered a wetland. It mattered not that the field had been ditched for over one hundred years. It mattered not that fifty acres of this farm was designated for wildlife in 1969 when the ditches in this field were relocated. It mattered not that the lawyer, the banker, the sheriff, the neighbors, the soil conservationist, and the widow Webster all thought it was a farm. It mattered not that I thought it was a farm and intended to use it as a farm.

Because such things as Disneyland, Cape Canaveral, the city of Chicago, etc., were built on wetlands, we now have a shortage of them so my hayfield has now become "public interest land."

I would also like to explain how a farm that had been continuously farmed had been declared a wetland. Mrs. Webster told me they maintained the ditches until the land was leased in 1978. The field was separated from the rest of the farm by the creek and the renters just didn't bother with it. By the time the now-widowed Mrs. Webster regained control of the land, the ditches had collapsed and formed swathlike swales that supported cattails because of the springs that fed them.

A large pine tree fell into Marsh Creek and between the flood trash and the beavers, a dam was created in the fall of '86 just below the ditch that drains the land Mrs. Webster still owns. The water then backed up this ditch and flooded both her land and mine with almost every rain until the dam was opened in '87. When I received the notice of violation saying I had drained one hundred acres and my field was only sixteen acres, I assumed I was getting credit for draining my neighbor's land also. When I received the letter telling me to plug the ditches, the diagram indicated my neighbor's ditch should be plugged. Then I was told the diagram was in error and the ditch common to our properties was the one I should plug. Since my neighbor regularly planted corn there, I told him I had to plug it but I didn't care if he opened it back up.

I was told about flood plains, pollution, and wildlife habitat, and I showed them I was improving all of them. Then I was told that the ducks which spend the summer in Canada and the winter in Florida used my field to stop over on the way back and forth. Much of the fifty acres designated for wildlife was used by the ducks. We had even bought a spotting scope so we could identify them as they migrated through.

The Game Commission is the designated Pennsylvania agency involved in the planning and accomplishment of Ducks Unlimited's wetland management program, and because D.U. believes it can control more land by regulation than by purchase, it follows that the Game Commission exerts pressure to regulate.

If wetlands are so important, and I've read that "our existence on this planet is dependent on wetlands," then the burden of maintaining them should be borne by the public. I see no rationale that dictates a farmer struggling to provide for his family should be made to bear a burden created by others. Nor do I understand the Corps of Engineers' selection process when the enforcement people ignore their own observations and prosecute on the information provided by the anonymous tipster.

On September 22, 1988, the D.E.R. mailed me a permit to clean and maintain existing drainage ditches in my field. On November 1, 1988, Jacob Sitlinger of the Pennsylvania Game Commission wrote a letter to the Corps of Engineers recommending I be made to keep the ditches closed. On November 7, 1988, Barbara D'Angelo from the E.P.A. wrote the Corps, "During the October 26, 1987 meeting, a representative of the Pennsylvania Game Commission informed the E.P.A. that the Commission had been interested in purchasing the wetland due to its waterfowl habitat functions and values," and she recommended that I be made to keep the ditches plugged.

When I researched my deed in the courthouse I found that I have recorded rights to maintain drainage through my neighbor's land as well as my own.

I do not oppose the government encouraging the protection of wetlands. If they would like to maintain the wetlands on their own land I encourage them to do so. When the government destroys wetlands to make a recreation area like Cowanesque and then tells me I have to give up the rights to my land, I certainly feel compensation is in order. If my land is more valuable as wildlife habitat than it is as a farm, I simply ask: Where was the Game Commission when this farm was sold in 1986?

Certain groups would have you believe I am anti-environment. This is not the case. In fact, if you would have held this hearing three years ago, I would have lined up with the Audubon Society or the Sierra Club. But now I simply believe I have the right to use some of my land to raise cows. If the Game Commission translated the twenty-third Psalm, it would read…"He maketh me to lie down in wetlands…." I for one feel more comfortable with the green pastures. As long as the Game Commission field people act as the eyes and ears for the enforcement agencies, I feel it is necessary to protect property owners from the myopic, biased, and sometimes erroneous information that leads to unwarranted regulation of private property.